"The Shrapnel Pickers"

or

"A Child's Eye View of the Second World War"

"The Shrapnel Pickers"
or
"A Child's Eye View of the Second World War"

George Schofield

Library of Congress Number: 2004099636
ISBN: Hardcover   1-4134-7828-X
               Softcover   1-4134-7827-1

This book was printed in the United States of America.

To order additional copies of this book, contact:
Xlibris Corporation
1-888-795-4274
www.Xlibris.com
Orders@Xlibris.com
26776

Contents

AUTHOR'S PREFACE

The Western Brothers, Kenneth and George, were a very popular radio and music hall turn in the 1940s. Dressed in white tie and tails, one standing and one seated at the piano, they sang, or rather "talked in pitch," through a series of comic songs, duets, and monologues, using an exaggerated upper-class accent. In later years, they ended their act with the same words in the same mock public school voices.

"Do take care of yourselves. There are very few of us left, you know."

I have taken that last sentence as one reason for writing this book.

It is not that there are so few of us left. We, the generation who were children in England during "The War," are still several millions strong, but over sixty years have passed, and memories are fading. Reminiscences tend to drift with telling and retelling, and usually towards the current geopolitical or social opinions of the teller and listener.

The time lapse between the event and the telling will also bear heavily upon the way a story is told, and not just through failing memory. Everything that happens to us in life over a period of years affects the way we interpret current events . . . and alters the way we remember past ones.

This is an honest account of my story as I remember it. All characters are, or were, real, although proper names are not always given. All events are true, and contemporary slang and vocabulary, accurate.

George Schofield
Connecticut
January 2005

INTRODUCTION

I, George William Schofield, was born April 1932 in a tenement flat at London Fields, Hackney, in east London, and within the sound of Bow Bells. I was christened at nearby St. Michael's and All Angels Church, and Aunt Edie was my godmother.

My father was a street bookmaker with a pitch in Goldsmiths Row, Shoreditch. My mother was, until her marriage, a forelady in Polikoff's boot and shoe factory, Hackney.

In July 1934, Father bought a new house, and we moved to, what was then, the leafy green London suburb of Walthamstow. "To give the children the chance that we never had," my parents often said. It was here their second child was born a year later.

About then, my mother's mother, who was an epileptic, suffered a stroke, so Granny Chapman moved into the new family house with us. She was paralysed down the right side of her body and could not properly use her right arm or leg. She walked by moving one foot forward and dragging the other.

It was soon after she came to live with us that Granny Chapman suffered a fit and fell head first into the fireplace. She lost all of her hair, and the burns caused her head to swell. The ointment that our family doctor and visiting nurse applied (hospitals terrified her, and she would not go near one) turned her skin dark yellow. I did love Granny, but for weeks afterwards, I was afraid to go near her, and for the rest of her life she wore some sort of headgear to cover the bandages.

It took over a year for her to, more or less, recover, but she rarely went out of the house.

So that was the situation at the outbreak of war in September 1939. The Schofield family of Dad, Mum, Granny, children George and Eileen, and dog, Peter the Painter, was comfortably installed in a brand-new red-brick three-bedroom semi-detached house, with garage and garden front and back.

Father's profession was never mentioned at home. His children were not supposed to know what their daddy did for a living. Dad left the house for work every morning at ten sharp and returned late, sometimes very late, every night. He was always smartly dressed in a three-piece suit and homburg and carried a rolled umbrella. A gold watch chain, and sovereign strung from his waistcoat pockets, completed the ensemble.

"If anyone asks," Mother would tell us children, "your father is a cabinet-maker's clerk.'" In our minds, there was nothing wrong with that. We did not know what a cabinet-maker did, still less his clerk. We did know that when Daddy left home every morning it was for his mother's house, where he used the front parlour as a sort of office. Granny Schofield's house was in Maidstone Street, Shoreditch, just around the corner from the Goldsmiths Arms public house in Goldsmiths Row where our daddy spent so much of his business day.

CHAPTER I

1st September 1939   Germany invades Poland.
11 a.m. 3rd September   Following an ultimatum, Britain and
                          France declare war on Germany.
11:15 a.m.   Prime Minister Chamberlain broadcasts
                          news of war.

Chapter I The Wedding 3 September 1939

When my Auntie Edie was asked by her intended to name the day, she made the mistake of answering the third of September! The church wedding ceremony started at eleven in the morning. The Second World War was declared at eleven fifteen.

We had to leave home early that day: Dad, Mum, baby sister, and me. It was Aunt Edie's wedding day, and a morning affair. The weather looked bright and sunny, although it had rained the night before.

"Stand there and stay clean," Mother ordered me after having been inspected and ticked off as ready to go. "Stand still, don't move and don't touch anything."

Our very best clothes were donned for the hour-long journey to Granny Schofield's house in Shoreditch. I wore my new, specially made, silky satin sissy outfit, in gold and black. My shiny black patent leather shoes sported silver buckles. It was no wonder I could not go out in the street to play.

Mother's diminutive figure was dressed in silver fox furs over a tailored costume, and she wore a new hat. She usually bought a new hat for special occasions, and as this was a church wedding, ladies were required to wear hats. My mum was known to milliners in every hat shop for miles around, and how I hated to have to go shopping with her. She would try on hats one after another before choosing. What a waste of time. Her new hats were chosen to go with her latest hairdo. Mother, so proud of her raven black hair, was welcome in many local salons, but she had only one favourite hairdresser—at any one particular time, that is. How I hated to have to go to the hairdresser's shop with her. What a waste of time. I always thought her hair looked better before she went in!

At least there would be plenty of interesting things going on at Granny's house. I liked to visit my other granny, a cheerful little stout lady, always laughing. But today the circumstances were different. Today was to be the big wedding day, and Granny Schofield's little terrace house in Maidstone Street would be full of big people.

When I say it was a little house, I do mean little. The street door led to a tiny entrance hall, front parlour, and a back kitchen downstairs. They called it the "street door" because it opened directly onto the street, and there was no front garden. This door was wedged open most of the time and shut only during bad weather and at night.

In fact, people in Granny's neighbourhood spent a lot of their days outside. When the sun shone, women moved kitchen chairs to the street and sat there, shelling peas, peeling potatoes, and gossiping with neighbours passing by. The weather would have to be very bad indeed to keep kids indoors. Rain or shine, the street was playground for children, on foot, on skates, on homemade scooters, or on "soap box" racing cars. The air around Maidstone Street (they called it "Maystn" street) was always filled with the shrieks and shouts of kids at play!

The house had no bathroom, but there was a flush lavatory in the backyard, just outside the kitchen door. Like other houses in the old street, a galvanized iron bath hung from a big nail high on the backyard wall, ready for bath night.

The backyard was just that. Not a garden, but a yard where nothing grew, and the soil like the outside walls of the old house, had been blackened by years of sooty rainfall.

As small as the kitchen might have been, it was always full of people. Since Maidstone Street did not lead anywhere, visitors could not claim they were just passing. A school at one end, with its high black walls, and a timber yard at the other, made it a sort of dead-end street. Just the same, neighbours and others seemed to be "stopping by" all the time. The teapot was always on the hob, fed with water from a black iron kettle atop the polished black iron cooking range. Granny did have a modern gas stove in that room, but she still liked the old coal-fired range. I had my own seat beside that fire too. Not a chair, mind you, but a brass box with a padded leather top, that was really a part of the fender. The box held brushes, polishing rags, and things, but Granny always told me that was my seat. Whenever we visited, she sat me there, fed me salmon and cucumber sandwiches, and told me that was my seat. I do not know how many of her other grandchildren were told the same thing. There were nineteen Schofield grandchildren, some of them already grown-up.

Granny often told that she had brought sixteen children into the world, nine of whom survived to adulthood. There were five girls and four boys—my father being the fourth surviving child, and the oldest boy. They were not all living in the house at the same time, of course. The eldest had married and left home, while the younger ones were still arriving.

It was Edith, the next-to-youngest daughter and last to leave home, who would be married today. Granny would be alone now that Grandfather was dead. Well, almost alone. Her eldest daughter, Ginnie, lived in the next street, exactly behind her mother's house, and they had made a hole in the backyard fence to accommodate the heavy foot traffic between the two houses. So Granny was not completely by herself as she still had the company of her daughter and grandchildren popping in and out, and there was our dad to look after on weekdays.

*   *   *   *   *

The younger women in the company were all talking excitedly.

"There is another wedding in the street today," they were saying.

"Lizzie is getting married today."

"Let's go and see how Lizzie is getting on."

"He stood her up last time, you know?" A group of young women, my mother among them, walked down the street to see Lizzie. I went along too.

A few of the houses at the beginning of the street had "area steps." We went down some steps to the front door, and into the front room. There, dressed in her wedding gown and veil of white lace, sat young Lizzie, alone and crying. Her tears left black lines down her cheeks, and that was confusing for me since I did not know about mascara. The conversation, as picked up by this little boy's big ears, made it clear that the wedding car, arranged by the bridegroom to take Lizzie to church, was very late, hence the tears.

The group were at first sympathetic, then advice from the girls came fast and free.

"He's not worth it."

"Don't waste yourself on him!"

"You're still young, you know?"

"Plenty of fish—" Just then, their unhelpful advice was interrupted by shouting.

"It's here!" a group of children playing in the street above was calling down through the half open door. "It's here; the car is here!"

A minor flap ensued as tears were dried, nose blown, dress patted straight, and Lizzie ran up the steps, into the waiting car and away, to waves and cheers from the group of girls left behind.

"I knew everything would be all right," said one girl as we walked back to Granny's house.

"So did I," said another.

*   *   *   *   *

One of Granny's younger brothers—the unmarried one— lived nearby too, on the other side of the street. Alfred Thompson, my greatuncle, an undistinguished-looking gentleman of middle height and late middle age, was only a few years older than my dad. He was an air raid warden, who had been away on a training course, and kept a "tin hat," in case of an air raid.

My dad was an important man in Maidstone Street, too. That was clear from the hullaballoo upon our arrival, with people on the pavement outside wanting to greet him and be recognised. That was clear from the group of men who seemed to follow him around wherever he went. Our dad usually employed three or four people to help him with his work. Mum told me they were "runners," so maybe they felt they might be needed at any time. Anyway, Dad was seen to have an entourage most of the time.

The house was full of excited people all dressed up in their best clothes, girls in Sunday frocks, men in Sunday suits with silk neckerchiefs, and best caps. My dad, like all the men in our family, always wore collar and tie.

The dining table in the front parlour was laden with food in readiness for the wedding party later on. The upright piano was in the front room, too, but it was always full of pieces of paper. Paper and money inside folded paper. I asked my mum why they did that, "Why not use a desk or something?" Mother only laughed and said they should use a desk or something.

*   *   *   *   *

The church was not far from Granny's house, just a little way up Goldsmith's Row towards the Grand Union Canal. Most of us just walked.

A small group of family members and onlookers had formed at the church door. This little boy's big ears were picking up snippets of gossip:

"Don't know what she sees in him."

" . . . now that other one had prospects . . ." Everyone agreed that my Aunt Edie was a beautiful girl. I could not see it myself even if she was my godmother, but there is no accounting for grown-ups' tastes!

We heard some friendly cheers as the bridegroom arrived. Wearing a smart double-breasted grey suit, he marched purposefully through the church door to take his place inside. My new uncle, Albert, was indeed a handsome fair-haired young man. I could not see anything wrong with him! We, who had been standing outside the church, followed him in, where we sat in our pews, and awaited the bride's arrival. This was an eleven o'clock wedding, and we did not have long to wait. Even so, Aunt Edie's entrance was, to me, something of a letdown. Instead of a white wedding gown, she was wearing ordinary, everyday clothes. I tugged Mum's sleeve and asked why, and was told to "shut up." Afterwards, in the street outside, she explained that

Grandfather had not been dead long enough for Aunt Edie to wear a wedding dress! Something to do with the mourning period.

*   *   *   *   *

After the ceremony, and after confetti had been thrown, everyone wandered back to Granny's house, where those with box cameras made people stand perfectly still, and face the sun, while they took pictures.[1]

We heard the tinkling sound of the old upright piano whilst still some way from the house. Someone must have taken out all the pieces of paper. The bride and groom were already there, and the party was in full swing with guests spilling out onto the street. Motor vehicles were a rare sight in Maidstone Street, only kids on skates and homemade scooters. Traffic was no threat to partygoers. Soon the company would swell still further as more people were to trickle back from the wedding ceremony. There were no written invitations for this party, as family, friends, and neighbours just "turned up."

As our mum used to say, "That's what I like about East End people—they are more 'free and easy'!" Mum was a Hackney girl, of course, and often talked about her own wedding. That winter day, some nine years earlier, when she and Dad were married . . . and from this same house. Then the party, she told us, went on for nearly a week!

Greatuncle Alf Thompson was not among the crowd forming at Granny's house. Now as well as being an air raid warden and an old bachelor, he was a joker and a prankster. Everyone was careful how they answered or dealt with him.

---

[1]   This wedding had no professional photographer; at that time and place, it was not customary.

It would be easy to fall victim to one of his many jokes, and nobody likes to look silly. Which perhaps explains why Warden Alf was not taken too seriously when he stumbled into the hallway, muttering something like, "It's started. The war has started!"

"Do shut up, Alf," someone snapped.

"That's not funny, Alf."

Alf did not wait to explain or convince anyone, but hurried off up the street to deal with other important duties.

When the enormity of the news was verified, the party wound down very quickly. The piano music was stopped, and the wireless switched on, as people just stood around. No one appeared to know what to do or what was going to happen. There were plenty of questions, most of them directed at my dad, who was somehow supposed to know all the answers. Today he was stuck for answers.

Aunt Edie stood sobbing in the hallway, as Dad tried to comfort her.

"Albert won't have to go," he assured her.

"The medical, he won't pass that."

"Anyway, it'll probably be all over by Christmas." His soothing words did nothing to stem her tears.

Our dad was certain that he would not have to go either. I heard him explain, "At forty, I'll be too old for call-up.

"Besides, I saw service in the army 1918-19, and boys service before that so I've done my bit. And then there's the medical . . ." Dad was sure he had a delicate stomach.

Old Granny Schofield was admitting to the questioning company that this would be her third war! She remembered the boys going off to the Boer War.

For as long as I could remember, grown-ups talked about the Great War (1914-18), and how terrible it was. About Zeppelin raids over London, and how they looked like "Big silver pencils in the sky!" About food lines, and the trenches, and shell shock, and poison gas, and all those boys who never came back. We had stood to attention for two minutes' silence every Armistice Day,[2] but to me it all sounded like a long, long time ago.

When people spoke of the last war, I thought they were saying the last war, meaning the war just past. It was years later, when I saw it written on a war memorial, that I realised they had been saying "The Last War," meaning never again.[3]

Although all those still at Granny's house looked sad and preoccupied, this little fellow could see the bright side of the situation. There would be plenty of cake!

*　　*　　*　　*　　*

It was late afternoon when the hired car came to take the bride and groom away to honeymoon. It was later still when an unsteady greyish green Greatuncle Alf was helped into the kitchen, where he sat down and was given whisky to make him feel better. He wore his tin hat and armband.

"A bloody fine air raid warden you turn out to be," my uncles were laughing. "The first sign of trouble and you faint."

"I did not faint," he argued. "It must have been something I ate!"

---

[2]　Until the outbreak of war in 1939, the two-minute silence was observed at 11 a.m. on every eleventh day of the eleventh month. Saluting guns fired, and everything stopped—traffic, people in the streets, shops, markets, and schools. Everyone respected the two-minute prayer.

[3]　The terms "First World War" and "Second World War" were not current until after 1946.

CHAPTER II

3 September '39	*British passenger liner* Athenia *en route Liverpool-Montreal is torpedoed and sunk by U-boat.*
4 September	*A fleet of ten RAF Blenheim bombers, with strict orders to avoid civilian casualties, attack German warships in North Sea ports. Five planes are lost. Germans suffer only light damage.*
September '39-June '40	*RAF bombers drop antiwar leaflets on German cities.*
9 September	*First six hundred Czech political prisoners arrive at Dachau concentration camp.*

Chapter II The First Evacuation

There was a loudspeaker van at the top of our road in Walthamstow, but I could not understand what was being said. The voice sounded fuzzy and far away. Groups of people were standing around their own and each other's garden gates.

The loudspeaker message became clear later when I heard Mother talking over the back garden fence to our neighbour, Mrs. King. They tearfully discussed the news that mothers and children should be evacuated, and we should all muster at Chapel End School. As I understood it, this was to be a trip—like holiday times.

The fact that Mrs. King and Mum were talking to each other at all was a noteworthy event. Normally they did not get along very well and had quarreled more than once. In private, Mum referred to our bespeckled neighbour, who always worked in a housecoat and matching mobcap, as house-proud. We thought Mrs. King even had a special outfit to wear when beating her carpets and rugs over the garden clothesline! The fact that these two were speaking like close friends meant the subject must be something very serious and important.

We, children, although not party to the family deliberations, heard about the plan afterwards. Mother, Grandmother, and we, two children, were to be "vacuated." Dad was to stay behind to look after the house and Peter the Painter.

✳   ✳   ✳   ✳   ✳

Chapel End, the local school, was only a ten-minute walk from our house. Along with Mrs. King and her daughter, Shirley, who was six, my mum, Granny Chapman, and little sister who was four and always wanted to be carried, some light hand luggage and our gas masks, we set off. Other people from our road were going too. We saw mothers and children leaving their houses and walking towards the school.

Gas masks had been given to us some weeks before. My little sister had a baby's brightly coloured Mickey Mouse one, but I was proud to have a black rubber, adult size S. Mother complained to the wardens when they issued it, but they answered that it "depends on your head size, not your age." So, with black rubber mask, packed in a rigid square cardboard box, packed in a soft grey sackcloth case with shoulder strap, and Mother close behind, I marched off to "vacuation."

As we passed the Tebbs family house at the top of our road, we saw that little Alan was upset. He was complaining to his mother about having a "floppy" gas mask haversack, and not a neat rigid square case like all the other children. His mother countered that it was his own fault for losing the cardboard box, and it did not make any difference to the function of the thing anyway.

We had been told to go to the school playground where transport was being arranged. When we arrived at the playground, the scene was one of complete confusion. Mothers, grandmothers, toddlers in pushchairs, bassinets, and perambulators,[4] babies crawling, and kids of all sizes playing, shouting, and running in all directions. There were Boy Scouts and Girl Guides, Wolf Cubs and Brownies, air raid wardens, WVS,[5] and a policeman or two. Everyone with a uniform was wearing it today.

The school itself was closed, or rather, it had not reopened after the summer holidays. Chapel End School was to stay closed for some time to come.

There was another group of people not in uniform, moving through the crowd, notebooks in hand. They looked like schoolteachers (since only teachers would attempt to bring order to this lot), taking names and addresses and distributing name tags. Every child, they said, must have his name and address written on a manila label and tied to his clothing. I felt angry and insulted.

"Did they think I was an infant who didn't know his own name?" At the first chance, I tore off the tag and threw it away. Every mother was also given a bus number to correspond with the bus we were to take when it arrived.

It was a long wait. We stood in the girls' playground near the girls' lavatories, a facility in constant use. We waited with Mrs. King, her daughter Shirley, and another boy whose mother, an acquaintance of Mrs. King, put him in her charge. The new boy's name was Morse. He was a kid

---

[4]   Baby push chairs.
[5]   Women's Voluntary Service.

about my size, and when our eyes met, I knew he was going to be trouble.

We encountered another neighbour from our road, Mrs. Trotman, with her two little girls. Well, she had other children but they were grown-up and not with her. Mrs. Trotman was a plump little lady, who looked and sounded like the middle-aged mother and housewife that she was. Mr. Trotman was a retired regimental sergeant major who had been away in the army, and their two older sons were in the army too.

Buses started to arrive at the school gate, and then followed some more confusion as adults and children tried to regroup. Our group was together as we found our way to the right bus. We did not know where we were going, of course, but this was the right bus.

The bus ride was a lot shorter than expected. In less than half an hour, we found ourselves at a Walthamstow railway station and more waiting.

When the train did pull up to the platform, it was special, just for us "vacuees." The carriages were of the old wooden "individual" variety—meaning, no toilet compartments—and the old smoke puffing little engine made hard work of getting us moving. Our train journey was a half-day-long affair, including frequent stops at nowhere.

The train was soon well into the countryside, and the first longish stop was at a railway siding, near an open meadow. All of the carriage doors opened at once, as children and others made for bushes and clumps of grass. Nobody knew where we were going, but everybody knew someone who knew our destination for sure. Rumours flew in all directions.

"Norwich," said one woman with her head out of the carriage window.

"Yarmouth," said another.

"I have it on good authority that . . ." Not even the engine driver and stoker knew our destination, or if they did, they were not telling. The women from the front carriages were out and talking to the engine driver, and word passed quickly down the line, "We are pulled over to let a troop train go by." In due time, a troop train did go by, as we all waved and cheered through our carriage doors' open windows. The long train, packed tight with waving, cheering, laughing soldiers, chugged on its way. Mother said, "They're going to war."

And off we went again. It was a good thing my mum and Mrs. King had brought food. It was like an "in carriage" picnic, and we all shared. Morse would not eat. There was nothing that he liked.

"What does your mother feed you on?" they asked.

"Sausages and red beans," came the serious answer.

We arrived at a railway station. Well, not exactly a station, just a platform, as there were no buildings of any kind in sight.

"Funny place to put a station. Nobody lives here," I thought.

On the platform stood two small Boy Scouts, with a large tub of drinking water. They handed cups to anyone who wanted a drink of water.

"What's the name of this place?" someone asked the Boy Scouts. The boys answered proudly with the name of their home village. Nobody was any the wiser!

Again, there was a mass movement to the bushes, and little bottoms were held over the grass embankment. My mum told me to go too, but I refused. That sort of thing is all right for young children but not fellows of my age. I was almost seven and a half!

As the passengers wandered idly about the platform, Mrs. Trotman, who earlier had been chatting to my mum, leaned over to her, pointed at me, and, in a stage whisper, said, "It's a blessing that they don't understand, isn't it?" But I did understand. It was an adventure. We were going to stay in the country to get away from the German air raids that should start at any moment now! We all knew about the horrors of air raids, from the newsreels at the picture house. We all saw how the Japanese aeroplanes drop bombs on Chinese people. But to a seven-year-old, the boundaries between the newsreel, next week's coming attractions, and the big picture are not always clear.

"Teacherlike" women appeared on the platform announcing that some families must get off the train here, and the rest to go on to the next destination. Names were called, and we got back onto the train. After some sad smiles, waves, and good-byes, off we chugged again.

The next stop was a real railway station with a newspaper shop, tearoom, and men's room. We waited here on the platform for some time. People said a troop train was going through and had priority. And sure enough, a troop train went down the line, full of laughing, singing, waving soldiers. Everyone at the station waved and cheered. Mother said they were "going to war." No one explained—if those soldiers were going to war down the line, how could the soldiers in the earlier train be going to war, up the line? I did not ask. Grown-ups can be funny sometimes.

New teacherlike women came into the station with a list of names, and the same thing happened. Some families stayed; the rest, including us, got back onto the train.

The next stop was ours. At Ipswich, we were ushered out of the station onto waiting single-decker little buses that drove off into the country. At one point, our bus left the others, and we travelled along a road that became narrower and more rural the farther we went.

It was late afternoon when we stopped at a farm gate, where two smiling ladies waited beside a small parked motorcar. Three family names were called: ours, Mrs. King, and another name we did not know. The four women, with their attendant children and baggage, got off the bus to be greeted by the two smiling ladies.

The road to the house was unpaved, rough surfaced, and unsuitable for their little car, they explained. We would have to walk the last few yards. We all walked—Mum, Granny, me, my little sister, Mrs. King, Shirley, Morse, the new woman who we later learned was a widow from High Street Walthamstow, and her three children, and the two smiling ladies who had waited to meet us.

The house to which we were led had once been a farm worker's cottage. Single storey, three rooms, plus kitchen and an outside lavatory. There was electric light and cold running water, but no gas and no telephone. The iron range in the kitchen was of the old wood burning style like Granny Schofield's, except Granny's was polished and shining with blacklead.

There was no furniture of any kind. The house had been cleaned, but was completely empty.

Oh, what a shock!

"No beds," they all shouted.

"How can children manage with no beds?" The mothers repeated this to their hostesses, and to each other. Their expressions showed disbelief, and some anger!

The two smiling ladies were a source of calm, as they explained their plan. Outside the house was a quantity of large *palliasse* sacks, and nearby, a haystack. We could fill the sacks with straw for tonight, and tomorrow they would return to organise the beds. Meanwhile, they gave each mother a grocery bag of condensed milk and tins of things— just for tonight, our rations they called it—then they were gone.

Mrs. King was not a woman to suffer discomfort quietly. Well, neither was my mum, but she did know when to complain and when to comply. Mrs. King, on the other hand, was unhappy about the whole situation and made no secret of it. As for the children, we all thought it was great fun, and happily helped with the *palliasse* filling, even if we did get more hay outside than inside the sacks.

The main farmhouse was nearby, and the farmer and his wife walked over to see us. An older couple, they brought cups, pots, plates, and things and told our mothers the location of the nearest and only grocery shop, bus stop, and public house. No, they did not have a telephone either, but there was a public box "not far up the road."

Everything to them was "not far." The farm was in fact only three miles from Ipswich—"not far."

The Widow Lady from High Street was very quiet, perhaps like my mother, still in shock from the day's events. She was a thin, pale woman, whose longish jet black hair was combed into no particular style.

That evening, after the farmer and his wife had left, we all ate supper, sitting on the floor. It was such fun.

And then we hit the hay.

CHAPTER III

Chapter III Country Life *Early September 1939*

Next day, a large smiling lady, in a tiny motor car, arrived to take our mothers to the church hall, which was, we learned, the nerve centre of the local operation.

Since nobody wanted to be left behind, everybody went. The little car took us in relays to the public bus stop.

At the hall, cardboard signs had been put up with arrows pointing this way and that. One such board read "Refugees This Way."

"REFUGEES!" shouted the widow lady from High Street, "REFUGEES!"

"I'm English. I've never been out of England. I'm not a foreigner!" She clearly felt insulted at the term, and it took some minutes for her to calm down.

My mum soon found the village store and a red telephone kiosk. We telephoned Dad; he spoke to my little sister and to me. Mum told him our address, and he told her that no bombs had fallen yet, and all was well. Mum gave him a list of items to bring with him on Sunday, when he planned to visit us.

Things were improving back at our farm cottage too, as furniture started to appear—a table, chairs, and bed springs; the women of the Mothers Union and or Women's Institute must have cleared their attics and cellars.

Billy was the Widow Lady from High Street's eldest. He was about ten, a head taller than Morse or me, and seemed very mature and authoritative. When Billy announced he was going exploring, a group of us, younger children, ran to fall in behind him. I ran to get immediately behind Billy and assume my rightful place as second in command, but Morse got there first. I tried to elbow in between them, but Morse only stood closer to Billy, blocking my way. I knew he was going to be trouble.

We trooped off in single file, and in order of height. As we reached the barn and fenced yard, Billy turned to face the line, pointed to the pig pens, and said, "There's a sow in there. No one is to go near that, the man said so." Morse then turned to me and the line and said, "There's a sow in there. No one is to go near that, the man said so." As he spoke Billy turned and walked on, and I pushed past Morse to take up my rightful place as second in importance behind the leader. Morse reacted by demonstrating his knowledge of swear words.

None of us knew it then, but this was Constable Country. This was Suffolk, by the rivers Orwell and Stour, the artist's dream. There were to be quite a few expeditions like this, implanting mostly happy memories of life in the country. Of rambling, tree climbing, berry picking, and tiddler[6] fishing. It was my first experience of life on a farm. We had traveled outside London before, of course, for summer holidays at the seaside. But looking at cows and sheep through a train window is not the same as being there. Now we were getting a real, if fleeting, glimpse at a way of life that, sadly, no longer exists.

One day my mum said we would be having potatoes baked in their jackets at supper that night. She had come by a bag of the big old spuds that roast well, and we put them in the ashes under the fire of the old iron cooking stove. Then our mothers split them open, sprinkled salt,

---

[6] Minnow or stickleback.

added a glob of butter, and we, children, sat on the floor to eat our fill of hot potato. The cottage still did not have enough chairs, but we enjoyed supper just the same. Well, most of us did anyway, for Morse would not eat it. Shirley King ate hers, but said she did not like it.

On Friday of the first week, Mrs. King announced her intention to leave. "Enough is enough," she said. Mr. King had informed her that all was normal at home, and that was where she was going. And early next morning, she left. Some of us walked with her party of three, including Morse, to the bus stop, and off they went, to waves of good-bye, to Ipswich station, and home.

We all went to Ipswich later that Saturday—my mum, Granny Chapman, my little sister, the Widow Lady from High Street, her children, and me. We put on our going-out clothes and went to town on the bus. Our mothers looked at the shops, and we all had tea in the town and were back at the cottage before dark. I liked Ipswich.

When our dad arrived next day, he was in a car with Aunt Edie and Uncle Albert, who had cut short their honeymoon. Their visit to us was brief too. Time for the grown-ups to go to the pub, which did not look like a real public house but more like an ordinary house with rooms. Time for Uncle Albert to strip the tree outside the cottage of its big green cooking apples. The farmer's wife said she was pleased the apples would be used; they usually went rotten where they fell. Then as quickly as they arrived, our visitors left.

My mum and the Widow Lady from High Street seemed to get along well. Like the day they went to the shop together and came back in a dung cart. Well, the farmer had warned them when he offered a lift, but they had misheard or not understood. Anyway, they both thought it a huge joke, laughing as they hurried to wash and change clothes. They retold the story over to anyone and everyone.

One day during the week, we went again to Ipswich. Mother found a café that served a "meat and two veg," sit-down dinner for only sixpence a head. My mum was good at that, so we dined out.

We, children, had not been told the real reason for the ride into town. It was to check the train timetable and buy tickets for home. Our mother decided to return to Walthamstow at the end of the week. And that is what we did, on the next Saturday. As the hour to leave drew close, the farmer's wife came over to say good-bye and offer us tea. Mother told me later that she thought the old lady did not want us to go. "Vacuation" had lasted just two weeks. Home looked just as it did when we left. No air raids had occurred, no bombs fallen, and Mrs. King was still next door.

Over the next few months, we sometimes saw the widow lady from High Street shopping in the market. Mother and she would always stop and chat. She, and her children, stayed at the cottage only one week more, before returning home. She confided in Mum that a gentleman friend wanted to marry her, but she had refused his offer.

Then we saw her less often in the market, then, not at all.

Some months later, Mother received a letter from her to say that she was happily remarried, and gave an address somewhere in another part of London.

We never saw them again.

Chapter IV

17 September 1939	*Russian forces, in accordance with German-Soviet pact of 25th August '39, invade Poland from the east.*
17 September	*Aircraft carrier HMS Courageous is torpedoed and sunk in Atlantic. Over five hundred are killed.*
27 September	*Warsaw surrenders.*

Chapter IV The First Air Raid *Autumn 1939*

It was early afternoon when my mother, little sister, and I boarded a number 38 bus at the top of High Street Walthamstow, on our way home from market. I liked the number 38 double-deckers. Some of the older ones had open stairs at the back, and if you dawdled getting on, you could lean over the road as the bus was moving! Today's bus was the closed-stairs type, and Mum pushed us inside anyway.

We had been shopping, but carried only a few grocery things in a bag. The afternoon was quiet. Few people or vehicles in the streets and only four or five housewives on the bus, that lumbered on for five minutes or so, before reaching the end of Hoe Street.

That is where it happened! The siren started to wail a chilling warning.

"Air raid, air raid," the bus conductor and women passengers were all speaking at once. The few people in the street were running in all directions.

An air raid warden appeared and ordered the bus to stop and the passengers and crew to take cover. At that time, London Transport double-decker red buses each had a two-man crew. A driver to drive the bus, and a conductor to collect the fares.

"What about our shopping bags?" someone questioned.

"Leave them on the bus," the ARP[7] warden answered. "I'll watch them."

We all stepped down onto the pavement unsure of what to do, or where to take cover.

Hoe Street Walthamstow was, and is, a main street with shops, pubs, and cafés. But leading off, on either side of the main road are narrow, quiet little streets with rows and rows of terraced small red brick working-class houses.

To the right of where we were standing was one such street, and about a hundred yards uphill, it forked into two to leave one house at the end of the line to stand alone.

It was not clear who saw her first, but one of our number drew attention to the young woman standing at the open front door of this house. She was beckoning to us and calling, "This way, come in."

The passengers and bus crew needed no encouragement. The firm grip of Mother's hand was on the back of my coat collar as we hurried up the street through the front door of the house, through the hall, a neat living room, and french doors to the backyard and . . . an air raid shelter!

The Anderson shelters were what you could call "semi subterranean," and in those months, a lot of people were having them installed in their gardens. The inside floor was about three feet below ground level, and the inside dimensions about six and a half by four and a half feet.

---

[7]   Air Raid Precautions.

Sandbags, stacked on and around corrugated metal sheet, made the roof and sides above ground.[8]

The Anderson cannot shelter many people. Six or eight full-sized adults standing up, and it was full, and at this moment ten or eleven grown-ups and two children were heading for the shelter. These were the women from the bus, all strangers to each other. The lady and man of the house, another young man family member, and the two busmen.

"Women and children," the men were saying. "Women and children in the shelter first."

And so it was. With the women and we, two children, down in the shelter, the men stood above ground smoking, talking, and looking for enemy planes. This unlikely group of people waited, and waited.

To children, grown-ups all look the same age—unless they are very old and grey, of course. So this little boy did not see any differences in the ages of the women in the shelter. Their conversation revealed otherwise—that the lady of the house was very young, petite, and newly married. The women were slow to chat at first, but as the time dragged on, they began to converse more freely.

The lady of the house put her head out of the shelter entrance and suggested to the man of the house that he "put the kettle on." Then she followed him into the kitchen to make tea.

On her return, she announced the tea was ready and suggested we go into the living room. The men assured us there would be plenty of time to run back to the shelter "if anything should happen."

The men stayed in the garden for their tea, while the now friendly group of women sat in the living room. Mother whispered to me to be extra careful as this looked like the lady's best china tea set.

---

8   By war's end, 2.25 million Andersons had been installed in British gardens.

The lady of the house showed albums of her wedding photographs, and the women "oohed" and "ahed" as it was pointed out who was who in the group pictures. And the lady of the house explained that her wedding had been brought forward as her husband was expecting to be called into the army at any time now.

And then it was all over. The all-clear siren sounded.

As the women said good-bye, they were made to promise to call again. The men all shook hands, and to waves and "thank you's," everyone meandered back to where they had started. We boarded the bus for home.

We learned later that no enemy planes entered our airspace; it had been a false alarm.

We passed that spot often, in the months that followed, on our way home from market. And I would say to Mother, "Do you remember when we went into the shelter at that house?" And she would answer that she did.

"And do you remember we said we would call on her again?" And she would answer yes.

But we never did.

Some years later, I noticed the house had been turned into a carpet shop. And later still, an office building stood where that row of little houses had been.

I always think of that day whenever passing that spot, and remember how a group of strangers, all ordinary people, were confronted with an extraordinary situation. They reacted in a very ordinary way, with tea and polite conversation.

CHAPTER V

1:30 a.m. 14 October 1939	*Battleship HMS Royal Oak is torpedoed at anchor in Scapa Flow. Over eight hundred are killed.*
November	*U.S. Congress approves "cash and carry"arrangement for sale of armaments to all combatants, British, French, or German.*
30 November	*Russian air force bombs Helsinki as Red Army invades Finland, attacking along its one-thousand-mile frontier. The first weeks of this campaign result in heavy Russian losses for no gains!*
13 December	*German battleship Graf Spee scuttled after Battle of the River Plate.*

Chapter V Christmas . . . *December 1939*

> *Stalin changes his socks several times a day . . .*
> *because he smells defeat.*
>
> —Music hall joke

We spent Christmas 1939 at Granny Schofield's house. Father Christmas left our toys at home as usual, but a bit early this year. Other children might hang up stockings to receive their toys, but not in our house. We always left empty pillow cases for stuffing and, on Christmas morning, always found them full. This year, too, the toys were plentiful. Hitler could not stop old Santa from calling at the Schofields. Our parents allowed us to take only one toy each to play with at Granny's. The rest would have to wait until we got home again. At my age, I strongly suspected the truth about Santa, but was savvy enough to say nothing.

Most of the family were at Granny's or, at least, stopped by for a visit. We had turkey dinner, and Christmas pudding with silver sixpences inside, and party games, and crackers, and paper hats. Everything was normal and as it should have been. Well, almost normal.

Only a few weeks ago, people were saying the war would be all over by Christmas. Well, here was Christmas, and our lives had not changed very much. There was the business of 'lights out,' a sort of halfway blackout, and sandbags started to appear around public buildings.

There had been no Guy Fawkes night this year. Fireworks were illegal and bonfires banned.

The BBC television service was discontinued for the duration of war, but that did not worry me. We did not have a television receiver anyway!

Yellow squares had been placed at street corners, and other visible public locations, to act as gas detectors. Each metal plate, about one foot square, was coated with sensitive yellow paint that was supposed to turn red in the presence of poison gas. I looked at them carefully, but never saw a colour change.

Fewer and fewer people carried gas masks wherever they went. And no one could be sure how many of those dressy cases some ladies displayed actually held gas masks. Some girls used them as second handbags.

Comedians on the wireless made jokes about the shortage of onions.

Walthamstow's council ordered the suspension of football games and stopped marking white lines on all its pitches. To deny landing space to troop-carrying German aeroplanes, trenches were dug across the grass. Not that I played football anyway, but I did like to go with Robby Maitland sometimes to watch his big brother play with the other big boys.

The major difference now was that many schools were closed. We did not have to, nor did we, go to school. I think this worried Dad more than Mum.

"He'll soon pick up when school starts again," she would say about me. As for my little sister, "School is not so important for a girl," Mother would add. "She'll only get married anyway."

So apart from spending more time at home, for me, everything was normal. Dad still left our house at the same time every morning and gave each of us children our penny pocket money. One penny could buy a bar of Nestle's[9] milk chocolate, or a lead soldier, or if I were to save the penny until next day, tuppence would get me a lead soldier on horseback! We did not know it then, but soon none of these things would be obtainable at any price.

Nestle's chocolate came back after the war, but not at a penny an ounce. Those lead soldiers and figures that I used to collect left for good.

Dad opened a fresh packet of twenty Players every morning and gave me the picture cards for my collection. I think he tried to make that packet last the day so as not to smoke too much. All cigarette packets used to contain picture cards. They were issued in series of fifty cards, and each series dealt with a particular subject such as motor cars, football stars, cricket stars, film stars, and warships of the world. The complete sets could be mounted in albums, obtainable from tobacconists. I had several albums full of picture cards. Tobacco companies stopped issuing cigarette cards soon after the outbreak of war. They never resumed the practice.

On hearing about the Battle of the River Plate, I took a heavy black pencil to the cigarette card collection and

---

9   Pronounced *Nes-ools.*

scribbled over the picture of the German battleship *Graf Spee*. That was my contribution to the war.

*   *   *   *   *

Each evening of that holiday, the family at Granny's would go off to the pub, leaving us children in the care of two young aunts who had babies. Aunties Ann and Lylie were wives of two of Dad's younger brothers.

We sat in the front parlour, Granny's best room, drank fizzy lemonade and told stories. When my aunts talked about their babies and vaccination, I told them I had been vaccinated.

"No, no," they laughed. "You were evacuated!"

The dining table had been taken out, but the piano was there and ready to make music for the pub goers to dance when they came back. There were no pieces of paper inside the piano; I looked.

The telephone stood on the dresser. Granny had a sort of built-in Welsh dresser to hold her best plates and dishes. Along with a glass dome-covered model of the Taj Mahal, the telephone took pride of place. It was one of the old-fashioned kind, where the earpiece hangs from a hook when not in use, and the mouthpiece is attached to the dial. It was all automatic; you did not have to ask the operator for the number you wanted. No, you just dialed the first three letters of the exchange, and then four numbers! I think Granny's was the only house in the street with a telephone, and that is why it was displayed so prominently. Mum told me it was for Dad's business.

Granny's house had electric lights and gas lamps, but I never saw the gas mantles lighted.

*   *   *   *   *

They must have started singing before the pub called "Time." We could hear them all as the family party and their friends reached the end of the street. They would sing at the tops of their voices as they walked from the Goldsmith's Arms back to Granny's house, and then the party would really begin.

Greatuncle Alf was usually at the centre of it all. He was the "life and soul" of any "knees up." There were so many stories about him that he became part of the family folklore. Like the night one of our dad's policeman friends called at Granny's house and stayed for a drink. But he stayed too long, drank too many, and had trouble standing up to leave. It was Alf Thompson, wearing the constable's tunic and helmet, who strolled up and down the street. In the days before walkie-talkies or cell phones were invented, or ordinary public telephones were common, policemen used whistles to summon each other. They say police whistles were blowing that night but 'ConstableAlf' was no help!

As I said, this story is strictly family folklore.

*   *   *   *   *

It did not matter if I could not keep my eyes open. Mum would simply take me to sleep in one of the beds upstairs. It did not feel strange being alone in a room in Granny's house, having stayed there so often. Besides, there was the noise of the party downstairs for comfort, if it were needed. We had visited this little old house so often that it was all familiar. I remembered when Grandfather was alive, and sitting in his high-backed Windsor chair down in the kitchen. He wore a hat all the time. Even in the house, he wore a grey cloth cap, over his bald head.

It was said that his long, varied, though not always successful, career had included spells as a sapper,[10] prizefighter, actor, and piano polisher. In his later years, he

---

[10]   A soldier in the Royal Engineers.

had helped my dad. Grandfather always gave us children a silver shilling at Christmas.

The last time I saw him was about a year earlier, and he was very ill. Sitting up in bed, in the little box room at the head of the stairs, he was wearing pyjamas . . . and a grey cloth cap. I knew he was very ill when he declined my parents' offer to let me and my little sister sing for him. It would have been for the last time.

I did not know it then, but this Christmas would be my last stay at Granny's house.

CHAPTER VI

February 1940	*Construction work begins on conversion of old Austrian cavalry barracks at Auschwitz . . .*
Night of 16 February	*Capt. Philip Vian leads two destroyers into a Norwegian fjord and captures German prison ship Altmark by grappling and boarding to free 299 British prisoners.*
13 March	*Soviet-Finnish war ends as Finland agrees to Russian terms.*
About 5 April	*The Katyn Massacre. Up to fifteen thousand Polish prisoners of war from camps in USSR are shot by MGB (Soviet Secret Police).*
8 April	*Note from USSR Foreign Minister Molotov to German ambassador on invasion of Norway, "We wish Germany complete success in her defensive measures."*
8-9 April	*Germany invades Denmark and Norway.*
9-13 April	*Five British destroyers attack ten German destroyers at Narvic, Norway. Two British and two German ships are sunk.British warships return to Narvic and sink remaining eight German destroyers and a U-boat.*
13 April	*British troops land near Trondheim, Norway.*

Chapter VI . . . And a Birthday *April 1940*

My eighth birthday was celebrated on Friday, 26 April 1940, by which time the war was eight months old. Even at that late date, our lives had changed little.

Foremost among the changes was school. We were still not attending classes. This time last year, the "School Board Man" would have been knocking at the door! He was the tall grey-haired man, who rode an oversized bicycle, to visit the houses of children not at school. He was no longer anywhere to be seen.

There were more uniformed men visible everywhere— soldiers, sailors, and airmen in the streets, on the buses, and at picture houses, and theatres. I was disappointed that soldiers wore uniforms in khaki and not scarlet, like the ones I had seen at Buckingham Palace.

One neighbourhood young man had died, in an RAF aeroplane crash. Our mum was so upset, although we hardly knew the family. Many funeral processions passed the top of our road, on their way to the cemetery, and black horses drawing a hearse was a common sight on Chingford Road. A crowd had formed by the time Mum and I took our places to see this particular flag-draped coffin go by. It had been some weeks since the young man was last home on leave, and I could no longer remember him clearly. I recall the day now because he was among the first of so many.[11]

Food rationing had started, but I did not know much about it. Identity cards had been introduced, but I did not know much about that either. The sandbags protecting many buildings were looking the worse for wear. Some of the sacks had been hurriedly filled with damp earth instead of sand,

---

[11] Over three hundred thousand British servicemen died in the war, and 109,000 from the Dominions and Empire. More than sixty thousand British civilians died in air raids. Thirty thousand of our merchant seamen were lost.

and now the rotting bags had split open. Some even had weeds sprouting out of them.

Shows at the theatres saw more waving of flags and the comedians told more "Hitler" jokes. Our mum and dad were great music hall goers, and we were regulars in the front stalls at the local "Palace" and "Empire." We stood to attention at the end of every show while the orchestra scraped out "God Save the King." Soon, we should, by law, have to stand for the French national anthem as well!

At the pictures, we cheered the newsreels when it looked as though the Finns were beating the Russians. Then they lost and were never mentioned again by anyone. The news also reported on the British army (BEF) in France, and we saw film of Tommies[12] digging defences for trench warfare. Many of the short films shown at cinemas were "information" pictures—such as how to use a stirrup pump, clean a gas mask, or what to do in case of this or that emergency. Some of these pictures had real stars in them, like Stanley Holloway, Will Hay, or Rob Wilton.

A popular song was "We're Going to Hang Out Our Washing on the Seigfried Line." Another was a parody of an earlier popular song, "Run Adolph Run." We had that record by Flanagan and Allen, before our dad ate it of course. The comedy shows on the BBC wireless had a war flavour too. Jack Warner was at Garrison Theatre, and we all used his "catch phrases." ITMA (it's that man again) used to mean Hitler, but now meant Tommy Handley. Even the quiz part of Ronnie Waldman's Monday night programme had more "army" questions.

For me, the biggest show of all had been the parade of the *Graf Spee* heroes. Dad took me to the "City" to see the march past in honour of the HMS *Exeter*, HMNZS[13] *Achilles*, and HMS *Ajax* ships companies. There were crowds and

---

[12] British soldiers.

[13] His Majesty's New Zealand ship.

crowds of people. Dad sat me high on a wall to see the sailors and marines and to cheer and wave my flag.

✳   ✳   ✳   ✳   ✳

I did understand that today's birthday party was to be a much smaller affair than some past ones. Like my fifth birthday, for example, which fell on Easter Monday 1937.[14] Our mum liked to boast that twenty-two guests stayed for three days! Well, they did not stay all the time; some went home and came back again. Others went home and stayed there . . . but new faces arrived, so their number and noise level was constant. They were all grown-ups, of course—no children.

I did not mind that the party was for them rather than for me. After all, they did bring toys, and the celebration was not entirely without children's things.

Our dad entertained us with conjouring tricks. He was good at that, our dad. One of his amazing feats was to eat a gramophone record! (He did not really eat the record. It was a trick.)

Mother got mad every time he did that.

"No wonder we've no music to play on the gramophone if you break all the records," she would loudly complain, but he would go on with the show anyway.

Then there was a big birthday cake, and jelly and ice cream, and on one afternoon, a picture show. A young man from the Crooked Billet came with projector, cases, and boxes of equipment. He pegged a white sheet up to the

---

14   On market day, Monday, 26 April 1937, warplanes of the Nazi Condor Legion bombed and strafed GUERNICA (Pop. 7,000) in Spain. The German-manned Heinkel IIIs, and Junkers 52s, attacked in waves between 4:30 p.m. and 7:30 p.m. Over 1,650 civilians were killed, and 900 wounded. The town had no military importance, but was spiritual and historical capital for the Basques. The attack moved Pablo Picasso to create his famous canvas.

dining room's garden door and windows. Everyone sat patiently waiting while the young man carefully wound and rewound his reels of film. His show of "one and two reelers" featured Charlie Chaplin, Laurel and Hardy, and the like. (Stan and Ollie were my very favourite film stars.) Mum brought in a lot of the neighbour's children, Robby and Sue Maitland, Clarence and Damian Snoad, the Trotman girls, Shirley King, Georgie Wildman, Josie Capes, et al. She packed them into the now table-free room and sat them in rows on chairs, benches, and even the floor. It was a good show.

* * * * *

No, this, my eighth birthday party, was to be a quiet affair by comparison. Granny Schofield was an invited guest. My other granny lived with us, so she would of course be there, even if she did choose to stay in the kitchen most of the time.

Mrs. "Mac" came. Mrs. Mac was Granny Chapman's only real friend. That was not her name; she was Mrs. MacSomething like McKay, or McDonald, but even Granny called her Mrs. Mac. She called to visit at irregular intervals. Well, on this occasion, she called to visit Granny, not knowing it was my birthday. She never brought a present, but I was always pleased to see her anyway. Mum explained that Mrs. Mac was a poor widow, and gifts were not to be expected. Mrs. Mac had been a widow for half of her life, but she still dressed in mourning clothes. A little woman, she always wore a black straw bonnet, and her heavy black skirts reached down to the ankles of her high black boots. Mrs. Mac was about the same age as Granny Chapman, and they had known each other most of their lives; she still lived in the same old street in Hackney. Their conversations were sort of continuous, with Mrs. Mac picking up her story of news and gossip, where she had left off last time.

Her story would go something like this:

"Mrs. Chapman," she would say, "I must tell you. Mrs. So-and-So has 'gawn'! Very sudden it was. Very sudden." Her speech was slow and deliberate.

"Well, I never," came the answer, followed by silence as they both meditated on the gravity of the news. "She married one of the so-and-sos from such a street, didn't she?"

"No, no, you're thinking of her brother; he married one of the girls from the other street . . . used to knock her about."

"That's right, she used to take in washing."

"No, no, that was Mabel, the eldest."

More silence as they both mentally regrouped.

"So Mrs. So-and-So's gawn."

"Yes, very sudden it was. Very sudden."

Let us hope that Granny understood it all, because I did not.

Odd in some ways, but apart from being a bit old fashioned, Mrs. Mac was a nice old lady.

One of her visits to our house coincided with a thunderstorm. Poor Mrs. Mac was so afraid of the thunder and lightning. She insisted that our mum hide all the knives and forks. "Thunderbolts are attracted to iron," she said.

Another time she was already there when I arrived home from school.

"Been to school?" she asked. "Then where's your slate?" Mum had to explain that schoolchildren did not carry slates any more, but used paper and pencils.

Robby Maitland, a boy my age who lived in our road, knocked at our door and said he had come to play. Well, maybe he did just come to play, but he stayed for tea . . . and did not bring a present.

Mother's cousin, Blanche, and her little girl Beatrice came. "Beatie" was about my little sister's size, and they would play together, and Aunt Blanche was funny. I mean she would do and say things to make you laugh. And they did bring a present.

Our mother had no brothers or sisters, and she and Aunt Blanche were close friends. Granny Chapman had had five babies, but only the youngest, our mum, lived past infancy.

* * * * *

As I said, my eighth birthday was a comparatively subdued affair. A pity, because it was to be my last party for a long time. There was a cake with candles, but after tea, everyone went home.

CHAPTER VII

10 May 1940	*German forces invade Belgium, Holland, and Luxembourg.*
10 May	*Neville Chamberlain resigns. Winston Churchill named prime minister.*
14 May	*Rotterdam city centre has been destroyed by Luftwaffe with heavy civilian casualties, even though city authorities have already surrendered.*
14 May	*Germans break through French line at Sedan.*
15 May	*Dutch army surrenders. Queen Wilhelmina moves her government to England.*
18 May	*Port of Antwerp, Belgium, falls to German army.*
About 21 May	*Sir Oswald Mosley and many of his British Union of Fascist Party members are taken into custody.*
28 May	*King of Belgium orders surrender of his army.*
27 May-4 June	*The Dunkirk evacuation: 336,427 British and Allied troops are brought from the harbour and beaches to England. Of the 861 British and Allied ships and small craft involved, 243 are sunk.*
8 June	*Evacuation of the last twenty-five thousand British troops at Narvic, Norway. In the final naval*

	engagements, the aircraft carrier HMS Glorious *and two destroyers are lost with over 1,500 lives. Lost with* Glorious *are two RAF squadrons of Hurricanes and Gladiators and attendant personnel.*
10 June 1940	*Over ten thousand British and French troops evacuate from Le Havre, and more from Cherbourg.*
PM 10 June	*With France nearing defeat, Italian dictator Mussolini declares war on Britain and France.*
11 June	*Italian air force bombs Malta.*
11 June	*French government moves from Paris to Briare.*
12 June	*Thirty-eight thousand French and eight thousand British troops surrender to General Rommel at St. Valery-en-Coux.*
13 June	*French government moves to Tours, and later to Bordeaux.*
14 June	*Soviet forces occupy Lithuania.*
14 June	*German forces enter Paris.*
15 June	*Verdun falls to German army.*
16 June	*Soviet forces invade Latvia and Estonia.*
16 June	*French Prime Minister Reynaud resigns.*
17 June	*Eighty-four-year-old Marshall Philippe Pétain takes over French government and broadcasts to the French people that armistice talks are in progress. He orders French army to lay down its arms.*
17 June	*British start withdrawal of remaining 165,000 Allied troops from France. The liner* Lancastria, *leaving St. Nazaire with five thousand troops and civilians, is hit by German bomber. Three thousand die. In the five weeks since 10 May, the RAF loses nearly one thousand planes.*
Evening 17 June	*In a broadcast to the nation on BBC radio, Prime Minister Winston Churchill said, "What has happened in France*

makes no difference to our actions and
purpose. We have become the sole
champions now in arms to defend the
world cause. We shall do our best to be
worthy of that high honour. We shall
defend our island home, and with the
British Empire, we shall fight on
inconquerable until the curse of Hitler
is lifted from the brow of mankind. We
are sure that in the end all will come
right."

18 June 1940   General de Gaulle, broadcasting from
London, says Free French would fight
on,and calls on all Frenchmen to join
him.

Evening 18 June   German army reaches Cherbourg.

19 June   Twenty-two thousand people evacuate
to England from Channel Islands.

21 June   The Polish government in exile arrives
in London.

22 June   French government representatives
sign German dictated armistice.

26 June   Stalin demands of Rumania that parts
of the northern provinces be transferred
to the USSR.

30 June   Germans occupy Channel Islands.
Russians occupy northern Rumania.

1 July   Marshall Pétain moves government and
names Vichy his capital of unoccupied
France.

Daybreak 3 July   All French warships in British ports are
boarded and taken over by British
forces. This includes two battleships,
four light cruisers, eight destroyers, and
about two hundred submarines,
minesweepers, and small craft.

3 July   Following an ultimatum—join us, go to
a neutral port and disarm, or scuttle.
British fleet off Mer-el-Kebir, Algeria,
opens fire on French fleet in harbour.
Two battleships and a battle cruiser are
destroyed, and over 1,200 French

	servicemen killed. An aircraft carrier, a battle cruiser, and five destroyers escape to Toulon, as does a cruiser squadron from Algiers.
5 July 1940	*Pétain's Vichy government breaks diplomatic ties with Britain.*
5 July	*Rumania joins German-Italian axis.*
5 July	*Japan occupies some French naval bases in Vietnam, French Indo-China.*
6 July	*German bombers hit Aldershot and southern England.*
6 July	*British-carrier-based planes attack Italian warships at Tobruk, Libya.*
8 July	*British ships and planes attack French battleship* Richelieu *in harbour at Dakar, West Africa.*
9 July	*British naval force including battleship* Warspite *and carrier* Eagle, *clash with Italian fleet in Mediterranean. Battleship* Giulio Cesare *is badly damaged.*
10 July	*Germans bomb ships and dockyards on English south coast. Sporadic air attacks continue until 13 August.*
21 July	*Stalin formally annexes Latvia, Estonia, and Lithuania into USSR.*
23 July	*Czech government in exile sets up in London.*
August	*In North Atlantic, a damaged U-boat surrenders to RAF plane. The U-boat is towed into port by tug and later recommissioned in Royal Navy!*
13 August	*Battle of Britain begins as nearly 1,500 German planes attack airfields and docks.*
15 August	*Over 1,700 German warplanes raid Britain.*
19 August	*Winston Churchill, addressing House of Commons, makes his historic speech: "Never in the field of human conflict was so much owed by so many to so few."*

19 August 1940	*Italian forces occupy Berbera, British Somaliland.*
20 August	*Italian air force bombs Gibraltar.*
24 August	*London is bombed for first time.*
25 August	*RAF bombs Berlin area.*
28 August	*RAF bombs Berlin area.*
30 August	*Massive German raids on RAF fighter stations.*
7 September	*The Blitz begins as the Luftwaffe makes massive raid on London docks. (These raids were to go on for fifty-seven continuous days and nights.)*
8 September	*Heavy raid on London's Battersea Power Station. One hundred and sixteen German bombers are shot down for the loss of forty-one RAF fighters.*
10 September	*RAF bombs Berlin.*
11 September	*Mr. Churchill, in a broadcast talk about the threatening German invasion, concludes: "We must regard the next week or so as a very important period in our history. It ranks with the days when the Spanish Armada was approaching the Channel—or when Nelson stood between us and Napoleon's Grand Army—but what is happening now is on a far greater scale and of far more consequence to the life and future of the world and its civilization than those brave old days."*
12 September	*Heavy raids on docks at London, Liverpool, Bristol.*
13 September	*Italian forces under Marshall Graziani invade Egypt from Libya.*
15 September	*Nearly a thousand planes attack London, Liverpool, Manchester, Southampton, Bristol, and Cardiff. A crashing bomber hits London's Victoria Station.*
13-16 September	*RAF (with Polish and Czech pilots) attacks invasion barges in French and Belgian channel ports.*

17 September 1940	The City of Benares, *passenger liner taking children and civilians to safety in Canada, is torpedoed and sunk in Atlantic. Thirteen of the ninety children survive.*
In the week ending 17 September	*Two hundred and sixty German planes are destroyed for 130 RAF machines lost.*
17 September	*A British naval squadron fails in attempt to land General De Gaulle's Free French troops at Dakar.*

Chapter VII The Billet and the Beer Cellar
May-September 1940

The Crooked Billet was Mum and Dad's "local." It was the big public house, not five minutes' walk from our front gate, which served as Dad's weekend social centre. The building was sort of modern rustic in style, which boasted a billiards room and dining room, in addition to two spacious bars. Unknown, even to most of the regulars, the Billet had a fair-sized beer cellar too. A haven that was soon to prove its importance.

Rustic wooden benches and tables outside the front of the building were used by thirsty patrons on summer days. Until two or three years past, there had been a big shady oak tree just outside, and on Sunday mornings, a silver band would stand there to play. But a need for more parking space brought about the removal of that fine old tree.

Mr. and Mrs. Lovegrove, the governor and missus of the establishment, were an oldish, plumpish, friendly couple, and I thought of them as jolly people. They always looked and sounded a cheerful pair.

Yes, the Crooked Billet was a high-class pub. The billiard room had played host to the likes of Joe Davis, and other top professionals, who gave exhibitions there. From time to time, boxing matches were staged too. I did not see any of this because the liquor-licenced premises were off limits to children.

The group of small-business owners and middle-management-type gentlemen, to be found at the saloon bar, formed the nucleus of my parents' local circle of friends.

Now the problem of licenced premises being off limits to children did not apply to private clubs, and just such a centre existed only a stone's throw from the public house. The clubhouse, and its sports facilities, was for members and their guests, but the term "guest" was very liberally interpreted.

The same group of customers from the saloon bar at the pub were, to a man, patrons of the clubhouse bar.

Of the two, I preferred it when my parents went to the club, rather than the pub. At the pub, we, children, would have to stand outside the bar door. At the club, I could play outside or, if it was cold, wet, or dark, go inside and eavesdrop on grown-up conversations. These always gravitated into two distinct and separate groups. The men, all standing at the bar, would talk about their work, the war, sports, or what they did in the last war. The war talk lately had been all about Dunkirk. It was mentioned in every grown-up conversation, and everybody knew somebody, or knew somebody who knew somebody who had been there.[15]

The women, all seated in one group in the main hall, would talk about rationing, women's ailments, what they had seen at the pictures, and each other! These women were sure that Dunkirk was entirely the fault of the Belgian king!

The club was a lot of fun, especially in summertime when they held weekend cricket matches, and our dad would often play lawn bowls on a Sunday morning.

It was on that summer the war really started—for us, I mean. It was then the sirens started whining for real air

---

[15]   Few British civilians knew about the Dunkirk evacuation until it was over.

raids. Not just practice ones, or false alarms, but actual German air raids.

As the summer wore on, the air raids became more frequent, until almost a daily event. People no longer ran for cover when the siren sounded; they were used to it and ambled along at their own pace. Well, they did around our neighbourhood, because nothing much happened. We heard gunfire and, now and then, saw aeroplanes in the sky, even dogfights, but the action was always some way off. That would soon change.

Our dad announced that we were getting an Anderson shelter installed in our back garden. And we did.

Granny Chapman took one look at it and decided it was too difficult to get into and out of. "When the Germans come, I'll go into the cupboard under the stairs," she announced. (On an earlier inspection, Uncle Alf had declared the staircase, and the cupboard under the stairs, as the safest part of the house.)

Mother did not look overjoyed either.

"It's got a dirt floor and it's full of spiders and things," she complained. "And when it gets colder and damp, why, we shall all catch pneumonia!"

I must have been the only one delighted with this new garden feature, imagining what it would be like to play soldiers and climb over those sandbags. It turned out to be a lot of fun.

*   *   *   *   *

I think it was a Saturday evening in late summer that we felt the first big air attack.

There was me, my little sister, and a couple of other children waiting outside the saloon bar of the Crooked Billet, when the alarm sounded. The siren was on a rooftop high post, almost outside the pub door, so there was no chance of not hearing it. The thunder of anti-aircraft guns was heard soon afterwards, and people started to move. Our mum and dad appeared at the door and led us into, and through, the bar, behind the counter, and downstairs into the cellar.

It was all new, unexpected, and exciting for me, never having seen this, nor any other, beer cellar before. Several dozen people were already down there, most of them familiar faces from our parents' circle of friends, and their children. Everyone looked cheerful and unconcerned. Some had brought their drinks down with them, and we sat on wooden benches or upturned small barrels. The big wooden beer barrels sat upon racks along one wall, with rubber tubes leading up through the ceiling, presumably to the beer pumps on the bar counters. Illumination came from bare electric light bulbs on the overhead beams.

The only thing I did not like about the place was the smell. A strong, heavy stench of stale beer.

Mother was more concerned with rats. She whispered to me that all beer cellars had rats! We sat closer together and slowly looked up and around in all directions. I did not see any, and neither did she.

The ceiling of the cellar was also the bar room's floor, and it must have been pretty thick, because not much sound from outside could be heard underground. That is why it is fair to reason that the guns outside must have been very big, or very close, or both. Some of those ack-ack[16] guns were mobile and towed by an army lorry, so that soldiers could set them up anywhere very quickly. The sound of the explosions was loud enough to rattle glasses down in the cellar!

"Not to worry," a gentleman, beer glass in one hand, stood up to explain. "Those are our guns firing back at Jerry.[17] They never fire straight up, always at an angle," he said, demonstrating the angle with his free hand.

---

[16]   Anti-aircraft.

[17]   German.

"If the guns are close by, then the Jerry bombers must be miles away!"

It all sounded reasonable, and reassuring to me, but there was something I had yet to learn about air raid shelters: Just as every Darby has a Joan, and every village an idiot, so every shelter had an expert!

Meanwhile, Mrs. Lovegrove was not to be intimidated by anything. Summoning her kitchen helpers she went upstairs to organise hot tea for everyone. She returned with the tea and some blankets.

"Bedding for the children," she explained, "They can't be expected to stay awake." The barmen had arranged wooden tabletops on the floor upon which the children were to sleep.

Kitty, a young Irish kitchen maid, was delegated to take care of us. The other mostly very young children were soon sleeping. Kitty and I took off our shoes and sat talking for a while, before we both fell asleep. We were awakened by my parents; it was early morning.

"All clear," they said, "Time to go home."

I realise now that Kitty was no more than a child herself. She just seemed very grown-up to me at the time.

*   *   *   *   *

It was still dark as we walked home. Well, I walked; my little sister had to be carried. We saw a lot of other people out and about, despite the early hour. Maybe they were going home too.

We had almost reached home when Dad spotted it. We stared at a small jagged piece of burnt metal, lying on the pavement.

"What is it?" we asked.

"Shrapnel," he said. "It's a piece of shrapnel." I picked it up for a closer look. This would be the first item in my new shrapnel collection, and I held on to it carefully.

As we reached our home, we saw that Granny was already up and about. The bed that Mum had made up in the cupboard under the stairs was uncreased, unused. Granny had defied the German air force and slept in her own bed upstairs.

"Peter," she told us, "hid under the bed all night long, because he don't like the gunfire at all."

*   *   *   *   *

My parents told me to wash and dress quickly, for the ride into the City to see Uncle Alf. They did not say why. The bus ride to central London was a long one, with lots of detours. Many of the streets around Aldgate were covered with debris and closed to motor traffic. Rescue workers had made pedestrian walkways as they cleared the roads. We were obliged to walk the last part of the journey and finally found Uncle Alf. He was wearing his ARP uniform with "tin hat," but this was not the laughing, joking Uncle Alf of old. This was a serious, tired-looking man.

In this part of old London the once busy thoroughfares were bordered by three-, four-, or five-storey Victorian office buildings with shops at street level. Today, many gaping spaces in the lines of buildings showed where bombs had landed. Most of the remains of the wood beams were still smouldering and turning to charcoal.

"This is from the latest raid," Uncle Alf was explaining to Mum and Dad. "They hit the docks, and all over the City and East End." The rest of the conversation I did not hear, having been deliberately shoved out of range!

I think this was a "take stock of the situation" excursion on the part of my parents, as they tried to decide what to do.

*   *   *   *   *

It was midday before we arrived at Granny Schofield's house. Dad and Uncle Alf stayed there, while my mother, little sister, and I set out for the bus stop and home. At least, that was the idea, but due to the bomb damage, some buses had been rerouted, and we had to walk part of the way.

We walked on through the Hackney streets until we came upon a crowd of people standing quietly at the head of a side street. What yesterday had been a row of shops and flats on the other side of the main thoroughfare was today a steep mountain of bricks and rubble. The only sounds came from the ARP men, hurriedly clearing debris in an effort to free whoever might have been buried underneath it all. The crowd was quiet and still. The absence of traffic that normally rumbled through this street added to the eerie sense of silence.

Our mum was not a woman to cry easily, but she was clearly upset by the scene.

"I knew that family," she said, looking towards the ruins. "Went to school with them girls."

*　　*　　*　　*　　*

In the days that followed, air raids continued and drew nearer to home. Some bombs had fallen on Walthamstow, destroying houses.

Bomb damage was not usually reported in newspapers or on broadcast news. The authorities did not want the enemy to know exactly where the bombs had fallen. This allowed gossip and speculation to have its way, and rumour is always bigger than reality.

We were lucky in having places to take cover during air raids. In the poorer parts of London, people sheltered in tube stations,[18] and even under road and railway bridges.

Many hours on various occasions would be spent in the beer cellar of the Billet, as air raids became routine events.

---

[18]　By one estimate, 175,000 Londoners slept in tube stations nightly in September 1940.

The usual refuge seekers were a jovial crowd. They could laugh and joke, and complain and curse Hitler all in the same breath. It was usually a happy experience to be there. One of the company would always be ready to entertain the rest. Sometimes someone would sing. Other times they would all sing.

Back at our house, there was something to sing about, too. Dad arranged for workmen to install a concrete floor in the Anderson shelter at the bottom of our garden. They put in a nice smooth cement that covered the floor, and four walls up to ground level, but no door.

"It's against the rules to have a door in an Anderson shelter," the ganger said.[19] Mother had wanted a proper door with hinges and locks, but it was not to be.

"A roll-down canvas or sacking, or a free-standing sheet of wood or metal," was the workman's suggestion. We settled for a sheet of wood that had once been the door to some old shed. The shelter entrance faced a six-foot-high concrete wall that separated the bottom of our garden from the sports field behind us. The old wooden door was not needed for blast protection, but just to keep out the wind and rain. We had yet to take cover or spend any time in our own back garden shelter. That was something I was impatiently looking forward to!

---

[19]   Much later we heard stories of people suffocating in closed shelters.

CHAPTER VIII

Chapter VIII The Second Evacuation
September 1940

Mr. "A" was one of Dad's pals from the Billet. He was in the car hire business and owned one or two posh, shiny big black motor cars that served at weddings and funerals. Although he was the business owner, he always wore a chauffeur's uniform when driving. He would salute, open the car door for ladies, and put a rug over their knees.

We did not have a family car anymore. Dad sold our little black Morris Minor just before the war, and that was just as well. Private motoring was no longer permitted, and only commercial users could get a petrol ration card. The few people who still had vehicles were ordered to immobilise them by removing the distributor head, and hiding it! This was a precaution against spies and saboteurs.

There were very few private cars to be seen on the streets, but one exception was the gas-driven car. Some people had converted their petrol-engined vehicles by installing a charcoal-burning contraption at the back where the spare wheel would normally go. This burner fed a big silk gasbag mounted on the roof. A full gasbag could be almost as big as the automobile itself! It did look funny, and the car was not very fast, but better than nothing, I suppose.

Sometimes, Mum and Dad would hire Mr. A to drive when

we went to Granny Schofield's house, but I do not think he liked that run. The streets around there were always full of children, and when they saw the big car, the boys would run after it to stand and ride on the running board! Mr. A would get mad.

* * * * *

We left home early that day, Dad and Mum, Granny Chapman, my little sister, and me. Mr. A, with his smart uniform and shiny big black motor car, was there ready and waiting at our garden gate.

We loaded our suitcases, and ourselves into the posh motor car. Other families were leaving by public transport, like trains and buses, or organized chartered charabanc,[20] but not us. The Schofields would travel in style! And off we went, over the North Circular Road, heading north.

It must have been very early in the morning. We passed people still out in the streets sweeping and clearing the broken glass and debris from the night before.

I did not know where we were going, but my dad was there in charge, and in the front seat beside the driver, so everything was all right. Mother was complaining, but then Mother often did. Under her breath when Dad was near, with less decorum when he was not. My only real worry was Peter, our little black-and-tan mongrel, back at home. He was so afraid of the air raids.

* * * * *

Our destination was Rushden, a small midland town. It is fifty-eight miles from London, and thirty-eight from Coventry as the crow or, as it turned out, the Luftwaffe[21] flies.

---

[20]   Anglisized pronunciation of *cher-le-banc*; a motor coach.

[21]   The German air force.

Our motor journey took three or four hours, including several "pit stops." We ate at a café on the way, Mum and Dad, Mr. A and me, while my little sister slept and Granny waited in the car. Granny did not like to be seen in public places.

Our arrival was an unheralded event, but it was not then clear to me why we had come to Rushden at all.[22] The place looked nice enough, with rows of trim houses and shops and everything, but we had all that at home. Besides, how could we be sure Peter would be properly fed and looked after by our neighbour!

We drove around the town for a little while, before stopping beside a row of neat houses, in a neat road, beside a neat park. Then Mum and Dad got out of the car and started knocking on front doors. Women in housecoats began to appear and join in the chatter with Mum and Dad and each other. Perhaps they wanted to help, or maybe they just came out to look at the new arrivals from London. This was a time when people still dressed up, not down, to travel, and we must have presented quite a spectacle with our fancy clothes and chauffeur-driven limousine. Our parents were asking these people if any had, or knew of, living space for rent for the two women and children.

One of the women, who introduced herself as Mrs. Hooper, told us that although she did not have a spare room herself, it was possible an acquaintance did. Mrs. Hooper scribbled a note and gave it to her daughter who hurried off down the road, note clutched in hand.

Mrs. Hooper invited us inside the house to wait and entertained us with tea and meat paste sandwiches. She explained that an evacuee was already staying with her. A Walthamstow boy named Gerald who was aged about nine. Her husband was a foreman at the paper factory, and her

---

22 It was much later that I learned about "twin towns." Country towns were paired with city neighbourhoods for evacuation purposes.

only daughter, Peggy, was almost engaged to a young man who was waiting for his calling-up papers from the navy.

Our mother, for her part, answered Mrs. Hooper's questions about London and the bombing.

When, at long last, Peggy returned, she carried another note asking that we go along to see the lady with room to spare. We all went along.

The lady in question, Mrs. "L," was the widow of a professional man and lived alone in a big house, in a tree-lined row of big houses. We were shown into the richly furnished large downstairs front room where old Mrs. L, speaking in her soft cultured voice, explained the proposal.

Mum, Granny, and we two children, could have this front room and use of the bathroom. There were camp beds in store upstairs, "If the gentlemen would be kind enough . . ."

So that was settled. Mum told me quietly that this would "Give us time to look around for something more suitable." Mum and Dad thanked Mrs. Hooper as she left, and she and Mum promised to keep in touch.

I do not think Mrs. L and Mrs. Hooper had met before, but they were both members of the same church group.

Mr. A and Dad had to leave early to beat the blackout. With street lights dim, and all car headlamps partially blackened over, only little slits of light beams were visible. All signposts had been removed from highways, and the public advised not to give directions to strangers. Posters everywhere warned us about spies. No wonder they were in a hurry to get home before dark and before the nightly air raid started.

As for Mum, Granny, and we two children, our new abode may not have been as warm or comfortable as the home we had left. On the other hand, we were safe from the bombing— or so we thought!

CHAPTER IX

27 September 1940	*Tripartite Pact is signed by Germany/ Italy/Japan.*
8 October	*Churchill announces reopening of Burma Road to China.*
14 October	*London's heaviest raid yet.*
16 October	*RAF attacks Kiel naval base.*
22 October	*Hitler meets with Pierre Laval, French deputy PM.*
23 October	*Hitler and General Franco meet at French/Spanish border.*
27 October	*In a speech in Brazzaville, French Equatorial Africa, General de Gaulle announces formation of the Free French organization—to free France and all its colonies from German occupation.*
28 October	*Mussolini's forces invade Greece from Albania (invaded by Italy Easter 1939).*
Night 28 October	*Four hundred and fifty planes attack southern England.*
30 October	*In a speech in Boston, USA, Franklin Roosevelt said, "I have said this before, and I shall say it again, and again, and again: Our boys are not going to be sent into any foreign wars."*

Chapter IX Rushden *September-October 1940*

Dear Mrs. L was more patriot than hotelier. She had volunteered to "do her bit" for the war effort by renting the room, without really understanding what was involved. The truth was the Schofields in general, and Mrs. Schofield in particular, were not the easiest of houseguests to get along with, and life in one room was no fun for anyone.

Going out to dinner every day was all right by me, but hard for Granny to walk to the High Street and back. I think she was also self-conscious about her bad leg. On rainy days when we could not go out, sandwiches were the order.

There was one High Street café where evacuee women with children would congregate on wet afternoons. The owner did not mind if we just lingered with an after-dinner cup of tea.

Luckily, meals served in restaurants were "off the ration," and not deducted from one's personal rations. At that time (Autumn 1940) good dinners could still be found in some public eating houses, although this changed as the war dragged on. By war's end, restaurant food was still unrationed, but the trick was in finding a café with anything worth eating! By then only fish and chip shops served palatable fare (Mother always said "fish and potato"), and even they would have a queue form as word got out they were "frying tonight."

There was an old cottage in Rushden's main street that was home to a good fish and chip shop. We sometimes took food from there to eat in our room back at Mrs. L's. Yes, we did have a tea-making "thing" and a dining table. It was a big round polished wood table with a tendency to rotate on its own. It was a good idea to hold on to one's plate!

Getting "more suitable" accommodation was not as easy as we had, at first, thought it was going to be. The little town of Rushden was bursting under the weight of evacuees, and rooms for rent were hard to find. The cafés, the children's parks, the afternoon picture shows were full of young mothers and children, most from London, but some were evacuees from other cities. They could recognise each other in the street and would converse easily and exchange news, ideas, and experiences. Listening to these women as they sat gossiping in the park, or wherever, we began to appreciate our own situation. At least we had a home to go back to. A lot of these people did not. Their houses had been bombed either before or after they left, and they had nowhere else to go.

Anyway, life for me was not so bad, playing in the park every day that weather permitted. One park at the north end of High Street had a *tank*! A real rhomboid-shaped British army veteran of the last war. It stood on a concrete base and was, I think, intended as a monument. The hatch was bolted shut of course, and kids would climb all over the thing. It must have taken more punishment from the little boys in the park than it ever did from the Germans.

Mother told me to make the most of my freedom, as I would soon have to go to school. She had mentioned school a lot lately . . . but was about to change her tune.

*   *   *   *   *

Thursday was pension day. It was the day we should have taken Granny Chapman to the post office to collect her old-age pension. On this particular Thursday, Granny was not feeling well, so Mum said we would go tomorrow instead. She had some matter to deal with at another government office. It might have been the food or identity card office—I do not now remember—but that was where we went.

As we approached the building, we saw some women standing on the pavement outside talking excitedly.

"It's an air raid," said one.

"Those are bombs exploding," said another. Yes, we could hear explosions.

There was one lone aeroplane in the sky, not quite overhead. Mum grabbed the back of my neck and turned my head up and towards it. "Is that one of ours?" she wanted to know. Since I collected model aeroplanes and picture cards, I was supposed to know. I did not, as one twin-engined bomber looked much the same as another up in the sky. So I stood open mouthed and silent. Mother pushed us inside the door of the building. As the women outside ran into the doorway, they met other people who had been inside, running out to see what was happening! No one heard an air raid siren.

Along with a lot of other nervous people, we waited just inside the doorway until it seemed safe to hurry home.

News of bomb damage was not reported in newspapers nor on the wireless. The authorities did not want to confirm the accuracy, or inaccuracy, of the enemy's bombing. Because of this, we only learned what had happened, in bits and pieces of information, over the next few hours and days.

At Rushden's town centre, just off the High Street, the post office, a cinema, and the school formed a sort of triangle. The cinema changed programmes on Mondays and Thursdays, and today was the turn of the cartoon feature *Gulliver's Travels*. My little sister and I had been promised a visit to the pictures to see this, and it was only after we arrived at the town centre, later in the day, that we learned about some of the morning's events. The cinema doorman came out and told the little queue of waiting children, "There will be no performances today."

"Why not?" one little boy protested.

"You will have to ask a policeman that question," came the sad reply.

The streets between the post office, school, and cinema looked clean. There was no broken glass or debris, but we did notice the school building cordoned off. It was clear the school had been hit, but we did not hear about casualties. Nobody seemed to know.

We were thankful for our own escape. If Granny had not been poorly that morning, we should all have been at, or near, the post office in time for the bombing.

Another casualty was the fish and chip shop in the High Street. We walked past the ruined cottage, and from the other side of the street, I saw the broken thick old walls. The heavy upper storey had crashed down onto, and into, the ground floor. We did not hear what happened to the white-haired couple who ran the shop.

The story spread through town next day that the German bomber responsible had been shot down.

*   *   *   *   *

The story of the bombing of Rushden, 10:15 a.m. on 3 October 1940, was reported in a local newspaper, but without naming the town![23]

This is what happened. A Dornier 17 became separated from its group and tried to make a dash for home.

Over the town centre it dropped its twelve incendiary and eighteen high explosive bomb loads, hitting shops, factories, an hotel, and Alfred Street School. Twelve people were killed, including seven children, three of them evacuees. There had been no warning siren, and the first sign of an air raid was the sound of exploding bombs. For that reason, teachers ordered children to take cover "under the desks," instead of in the school shelter outside. One master, Mr. Hales, told his class to sing—whilst crouched under desks. Then the headmaster, Mr. Lawrence, ordered a calm retreat to the shelter.

---

[23] This account of the attack is taken from that newspaper report, articles published by Rushden History Society, and eyewitness accounts recorded at Heritage House, Rushden.

Only one teacher was visibly distressed—the lady whose class of infants had been at the centre of the explosion.

The fish and chip shop proprietor survived the bombing. His wife did not.

The bomber was shot down by RAF fighters. The German pilot survived the crash but died later in hospital.

CHAPTER X

3 November 1940	*For the first night since 7 September, there was no air raid over London. Since the "Battle of Britain" began, over two thousand German planes have been shot down.*
5 November	*A thirty-seven-ship convoy is attacked in mid-Atlantic by German battleship Admiral Scheer. The armed merchantman* Jervis Bay *engages the battleship long enough for thirty-two of the ships to escape.*
7 November	*RAF bombs Krupp factories at Essen.*
8 November	*Anniversary of the Munich "putsch." RAF raid cuts short Hitler's speech!*
9 November	*Death of Neville Chamberlain from cancer.*
11 November	*First mass execution of fifty-five Polish intellectuals at Dachau concentration camp.*
11 November	*Twenty-one planes from carrier* Illustrious, *with seaplanes from Malta, attack Italian fleet anchored at Taranto naval base. Three of Mussolini's battleships plus two cruisers plus smaller ships plus dock installations are badly damaged, for the loss of two British planes. (It has been said by several experts that this torpedo attack in a shallow well-protected harbour*

	gave Japan the "inspiration" for Pearl Harbour.)
14 November 1940	Coventry "fire bombed." Five hundred and seventy civilians are killed in this one raid.
15 November	Greeks advance into Albania as Italians retreat.
16 November	RAF raids Hamburg.
21 November	News that Greek forces advancing further into Albania take two thousand Italian prisoners, capture hundreds of guns.
23 November	Southampton is heavily bombed.
24 November	Slovakia joins Axis Pact.
5 December	Sidi Barrani, Egypt, falls to Dominion forces.
7 December	RAF bombs Düsseldorf.
8 December	Twenty-five thousand Dominion/British/ Indian troops under General O'Connor attack Italian front in Egypt.
12 December	Sheffield is bombed.
December	A U.S. warship is sent to Capetown to collect British gold as prepayment for war materials and armaments to be made available to Britain.

Chapter X Rushden 2 *November-December 1940*

We did keep in touch with the Hoopers and visited them from time to time. Theirs was a happy house, often graced by visitors. It was like Granny Schofield's, with friends and family always stopping by. The conversations, like the Hoopers parlour, were warm and cheerful. Gerald, the Walthamstow evacuee, was particularly in awe of our mum for having actually been to Germany! He asked lots of questions.

It was like this: Dad took Mum to the continent to see the places he had seen in the army. They also toured in Belgium and the French channel coast. This was at a time (about 1930) when very few ordinary English people traveled to

Europe. It always caused a stir when mentioned in casual conversation, which Mum often did.

*   *   *   *   *

Mother was not what you would call a talkative woman, but she did somehow make friends easily. As we got to know the town better, she became part of a circle of women, mostly evacuees, some locals, all chatty.

One odd thing about Rushden was the lack of pubs. Maybe they were there, but I just did not notice. It was unlike some London neighbourhoods where the public house was a prominent feature of every other street corner. No, in this town, the drinking classes did their socializing in clubs, not pubs.

I may be wrong, but these "social" clubs appeared to belong to factories, businesses, and such, and existed for the benefit of their own employees. If that were so, then everyone used everyone else's club, because people wandered in and out of them unchallenged.

We were soon introduced to our first club. Our mum and we, two little ones, were taken by a local couple early one evening to a place in or near the High Street. We sat at a table, ordered drinks from the waiter, and awaited the cabaret.

A blind man with a piano accordion was led into the middle of the floor, where he stood and played a medley of popular songs. Then he was led off.

There was a long wait before two thin little adolescent girls, wearing sequined dance costumes and tap shoes, took to the floor. With self-conscious expressions, they sang a song, did a tap dance, and made their exit. There was another long wait until the accordion player returned, and the process started over again.

This was not the Hackney Empire, nor even the Walthamstow Palace, but it was live entertainment. Sitting there, sipping my glass of spruce (a fizzy, sweet dark red soft drink), I felt very sophisticated, very important, very grown-up.

This was a respectable establishment where unaccompanied ladies could go, our new friends explained to Mother. But I do not think we ever went back alone. We did return there once when Dad was visiting Rushden. The same cabaret artists were still on the bill!

*   *   *   *   *

Our primary entertainment was the cinema, and the town had three or four good picture palaces. Granny did not like the pictures, so even with that we had a problem.

"Talkies always give me a headache," she said. Granny did not hear well, or see well, so I supposed the picture show would give her a headache. Sometimes she would consent to go with us, but usually we had to take her home first.

Only once did she enjoy a picture. It was an Old Mother Riley comedy, and in those slapstick-cum-pathos films, Mother Riley was always the victim who triumphs in the end.

I did hope Granny was not identifying herself with Mother Riley.

Another diversion was the idea of a local church minister. He organized a "Happy Hour" in the church hall for evacuee mothers with young children. Tuppence (2d) for an afternoon cup of tea and biscuit, toys and games for the babies.

We went there once only. Our mum did not like churches or anything to do with them. "Hypocrites, that's what churchgoers are," she would say. "All hypocrites!" As far as she was concerned, the church was for christenings, weddings, and funerals, and should be otherwise avoided. So we did.

*   *   *   *   *

Gerald, Mrs. Hooper's young evacuee, went home to Walthamstow when his mother came and took him. That left room for us at the Hooper house.

When our mum announced she would have to go home to Walthamstow for a week or two, Granny, little sister, and me, moved to the Hoopers. It was a temporary arrangement, but it did mean we should not have to go out to dinner anymore, and Granny could stay indoors all the time. While we were in this house, Mrs. Hooper would prepare all meals.

A patient lady was Mrs. Hooper, who would take the time to explain things. She would read to us children from her illustrated book of Bible stories, pointing to the pictures as she went, and carefully answering our questions.

We were introduced to the ferret in its cage outside the back door. Mr. Hooper used to go out hunting rabbits with that animal. He had promised to take me with him sometime. But he never did.

We were shown the family car, too. It was in its wooden garage out the back, all covered and greased. Parts of the engine had been taken out and hidden, "So the Germans can't use it," we were told.

"As soon as the war is over, we shall all go for a ride," Mrs. Hooper added.

*   *   *   *   *

There was, of course, still the problem of Granny Chapman's epileptic fits, which our mum, in her haste, had neglected to mention to our new landlady. It was no problem at all for us children. Even my little sister, who was only five, knew exactly what to do in case Granny had a fit. We had seen it so often before that it was a routine event.

As soon as Granny started a fit, we would make sure she could not hurt herself in a fall. I mean we moved furniture and any hot, or sharp things out of her way. A "normal" epileptic should be given something to bite on, to prevent biting off the tongue. We, little ones, were not strong enough to do anything about that, and Gran did not have many teeth anyway. So we would just stay near her until the fit had passed, and she regained her senses and composure. The whole episode took no more than five or ten minutes, before we returned to our games, or whatever we had been doing.

On this particular afternoon, Granny was sitting in the corner armchair, her indoor shawl over her shoulders, and we, children, at the table when it started. Poor old Granny went into convulsions and shaking. When she began dribbling and rocking slowly to and fro, we knew this was another fit. My little sister looked at me, and her expression asked, "Should we do something?" I looked back at her, and my expression must have answered "No, she's in the armchair and can't fall." So we did nothing.

We forgot that poor Mrs. Hooper was not a party to our sign language, and she began to panic! "What is it? What's happening? Fetch the brandy," she called to her daughter, Peggy.

We, children, tried to explain, "It's only a fit. Everything is all right. Granny will be better in a minute." Although we spoke together, we did not speak in unison, which further complicated the situation! I did not mention it, but alcohol was not a good idea for Granny, at that moment.

Peggy arrived with the brandy, which was kept in the first-aid cabinet. Its tatty label suggested it had been there a long time, since the Hoopers were not exactly drinking people.

I need not have worried about alcohol, as the brandy was for Mrs. Hooper who was feeling rather faint!

"Better not to worry about it," I thought. Mother would be with us in a few days, and she can explain everything!

*   *   *   *   *

A few days later, our mum returned, and she had Peter with her. My joy at seeing our dog again evaporated quickly when she explained the reason for bringing him.

"Peter," she told me later when we're alone, "will have to be destroyed. There is nowhere to keep him here, and in London he is terrified of the air raids. It is cruelty to keep him."

Even as I protested and argued, I knew that she was right. This was the news I had feared for a long time. There just was no place for poor Peter anymore. He was one more war victim.

That night, I tried to enlist the support of my little sister, but when the word "kill" was mentioned, she snapped back, "Peter is not going to be killed. He is being put to sleep. Mummy said so."

You cannot argue with that!

I was not going to cry—that was for sure. My mind was made up.

The next night, a man came to the house. He was some hunting fellow that Mr. Hooper knew. A weather-beaten-looking man in oilskin coat and rubber boots. He tied one end of a piece of string around Peter's neck to lead him away. Mother gave the man five shillings.

I did not cry. Not then.

CHAPTER XI

January 1941	*Over a hundred shelterers are killed when London's BANK tube station suffers a direct hit.*
January	*British Communist Party newspaper, the* Daily Worker, *is banned by House of Commons, vote 297 to 11.*
1 January	*British/Australian troops with strong naval and air support attack Bardia, Libya.*
5 January	*Bardia falls.*
10 January	*Aircraft carrier HMS* Illustrious *and cruiser HMS* Southampton *are badly damaged, and two transport ships are sunk by German Stukas (dive-bombers) based in Sicily.*
11 January	*RAF bombs Luftwaffe bases in Sicily. (Axis warplanes based in Sicily and southern Italy effectively close the eastern Mediterranean to British supply ships. British forces in Egypt and the Middle East are supplied by way of the Cape of Good Hope.)*
16 January	*Large force of German dive-bombers attack Valeta harbour, Malta, where HMS* Illustrious *is undergoing repairs.*
19 January	*British forces attack Italians in Somaliland, Eritrea, and Abyssinia.*
22 January	*British/Australian troops take Tobruk.*

27 January 1941	British/Indian forces take Agordat, Eritrea.
29 January	Italian forces abandon Derna, Libya.
February	General Rommel appointed Commander Afrika Corps.
5 February	Mussolini's forces suffer heavy losses at Beda Fomm, Libya.
6 February	Australian troops take Benghazi. Seven German generals among the many prisoners.
7 February	Italian General Berganzoli surrenders at Beda Fomm, twenty thousand prisoners taken. By end February 1941, all Cyrenaica is under Eighth Army control; 130,000 prisoners, 400 tanks, and 1,300 guns are captured since campaign began 5 December.
9 February	Naval forces under Admiral Somerville bomb and shell Genoa docks.
1 March	Bulgaria joins Axis.
5 March	First British troops arrive in Greece.
25 March	Yugoslavia signs Tripartite Pact and joins Axis.
25 March	Italian torpedo boats attack British ships in Suda Bay, Crete. Cruiser HMS York is badly damaged.
25 March	German troops under General Rommel retake El Agheila from British and advance eastward.
27 March	British force Italian army out of Keren, Eritrea.
27 March	Rioting in Yugoslavia against signing of Axis Pact. Government is overthrown in favour of seventeen-year-old King Peter. New government scraps pact.
27-28 March	Battle of Matapan. Major defeat for Mussolini's navy as five cruisers and three destroyers are sunk, and 2,400 Italians are killed. British fleet led by Admiral Cunningham on HMS Warspite suffers no losses. (Aboard the battleship

	HMS Valiant *serves a junior officer—*
	Philip Mountbatten.)
2 April 1941	*Rashid Ali and his pro-Nazi supporters*
	take over Irak and close oil pipeline to
	Mediterranean.
2 April	*Four of five Italian destroyers en route*
	Port Sudan are sunk by British torpedo
	bombers.

Chapter XI Rushden 3 *December 1940-March 1941*

How we met Mr. and Mrs. "B," in the first place, is no longer clear to me. They were Rushden people. A middle-aged couple without children, who described themselves as "rough and ready." That was the phrase Mrs. B used often, and a phrase that appealed to our mum, who was not altogether comfortable around people who were not, as she put it, 'rough and ready.'

Perhaps I would have paid more attention to our new friends had it been known we were going to move in with them. Mother took Granny home to our house in Walthamstow, and when she came back, we moved in with the Bs. We remained friends with the Hoopers and still visited with them, but our stay there had been a temporary arrangement anyway.

Granny Chapman was to hold the fort at home and look after Dad. She made it clear that, bombs or not, home was where she wanted to be. Granny had suffered enough from evacuations.

*   *   *   *   *

Mother and we, two children, took the upstairs master bedroom in our new lodgings. My clear memories of that house were good dinners and cold, cold beds. Cold beds mean disturbed, uneasy sleep and nightmares! Mrs. B seemed to consider a warm bedroom somehow sinful.

Luckily our stay there was to be brief. As experts explained it afterwards, "Two women into one kitchen won't go!"

This little terrace house was in a poorer part of town, in a street of other houses exactly like it. The front door opened directly onto the pavement, just like Granny Schofield's in Shoreditch.

Staying with Mr. and Mrs. B without Granny did mean that we could go out more easily. One evening we went to the pictures with Mrs. B. We sat through the advertisements and the coming attractions. In the newsreel, there were pictures of Mr. Churchill inspecting bomb damage in London. The audience burst into applause and cheers when he came on to the screen. They usually did.

The problem came during the supporting film. A sign was flashed on to the screen, "ALERT, the air raid alarm has been sounded." This was a common occurrence in cinemas at home nowadays but a rare event in Rushden. Most people just stayed seated where they were. As our mum would say, "We could be killed just as easily outside as inside the picture house!" It was clear from her agitated state that Mrs. B did not share our mum's philosophy. She was all of a flutter and insisted we leave the theatre. So we did.

Outside in the street, all looked and sounded quiet and peaceful. There was no action or gunfire to be heard, and people were walking and behaving normally. It was not a false alarm, just a non-event.

"That's the last time we go to the pictures with her," Mother whispered to me. "She's too nervous!"

What was worse, it was a cowboy picture that we had missed!

*　　*　　*　　*　　*

We went home for Christmas 1940, but everything was not entirely normal nor as I thought it should have been. Our house had a cold, damp, unlived-in feel about it.

"The Shrapnel Pickers" or "A Child's Eye View of the Second World War"

Even the two aspidistras in our front parlour were dead and standing shrunken, brown, and lifeless. Each in its big glazed jardinière, atop a dark wood stand decorated with inlaid marquetry. They had flanked the big front bay window like two sentries on guard. And to think they were once Mother's pride!

We stayed the whole week and a bit. There was not much enemy action that week. The siren sounded a few times, but no bombs fell near our house.

Four made-to-measure bunks had been delivered for our Anderson shelter in the back garden. The thick wooden frames with flat metal strips, woven into big squares, supported the thin mattresses. I was sort of hoping for an air raid so that we could sleep in our shelter, but there wasn't, and we didn't.

I did find a hole in a bathroom window and went running to report it.

"Dad, Dad, there's a bullet hole in the bathroom window upstairs!"

"No," he explained. "Not a bullet hole, but a shrapnel hole. I found the piece of metal in the bathtub, and saved it for you," he said.

My shrapnel collection was growing, but toys and presents were not so plentiful this year. Nothing this year was as good as in years past.

A lot of our neighbours were away from home, and our road had an empty feel about it. Many homes had strips of sticky paper on their windows to stop glass splinters flying in an explosion. Others had black paper or curtains permanently on the windowpanes to stop any light from showing through. It gave them an abandoned look that the blackout did nothing to improve. Streetlights were so dim they almost did not count. People out at night carried electric torches to see the way up and down kerbstones, steps, and things.

The Billet and the club were still there, but even these had a dismal look about them.

This Christmas had been a sad disappointment. We, children, were allowed to carry one toy back with us to Rushden. I chose my spinnable globe of the world. It was not a new toy, but an old favourite. My little sister picked a doll.

* * * * *

Mrs. B cooked North Country style. Sunday dinner always started with gravy-covered Yorkshire pudding as a separate dish, followed by the main course, of roast meat with vegetables, then nothing. She did not believe in serving "afters" (dessert) on a Sunday, the rest of the week yes, but never on Sunday.

I could get along with that routine. It was the cold upstairs rooms of the house that I did not like. Only downstairs had heating, and in bed I shivered.

* * * * *

More evacuees were still arriving in town, and it was hard to see where they were going to put them all. For example, one day, walking with my mother near the bus garage, we caught up with two young women. They were ambling along at a snail's pace, each carrying a heavy-looking suitcase. They were both thin, shabbily dressed, and turning blue with cold. They were a sorry sight, and as we drew near enough to hear them speak to each other, we realized they were . . . Cockneys!

"What's the matter?" Mother asked them, "Ain't you got nowhere to go?"

They started to tell their story to our mum, how they had left London and just taken a chance on finding somewhere to stay. Now they did not know who or where to ask.

"Did you come by bus?" Mother asked.

They were nodding yes.

"Did you notice the café at the bus station?"

They were nodding no.

"Well, you can't miss it. It's part of the building. Go in there and ask for . . . ," Mum told them the name of the woman in charge. "She keeps a list. She will help you."

The two girls thanked our mum and went off in the direction they were told.

"We didn't want to get too involved," Mum said to me when they had gone. "You never know, they might be here just to pick up soldiers!"

Mum hesitated and thought for a moment. "Oh, I don't know, I can't imagine many soldiers would fancy them two!"

*   *   *   *   *

It was true that on weekends the town would be full of men in uniform. Mostly army khaki, but some air force blue. Many of the soldiers were really "Home Guard." The uniform was just like the army's, except for the words "Home Guard" on the shoulder. These civilian men of military age were required to train with the "Guard" for a certain number of hours each week. On weekends the local club bars would be full of them.[24]

Now that I was collecting regimental badges, my interest was in looking at these army cap insignia. A wide array of military units could be seen in the High Street, on a Saturday evening. Once I saw a soldier wearing a revolver in a half holster. It was the first time I had ever seen a real gun. Mum said she thought he had no business carrying the thing, and the young man was only showing off!

*   *   *   *   *

When the inevitable quarrel with Mrs. B came, our mum announced that we were leaving. She took me and my little

---

[24]   By the end of 1941, the Home Guard was one million strong nationwide.

sister over to the Hoopers and then went home. I was given strict instructions to, "Look after your sister, do as you are told, and behave yourself!" And off she went to our house in Walthamstow to Dad and to Granny.

Mrs. Hooper made her plans clear right away.

"It's school for you, young man. Monday morning and you are going to school." I had mixed feelings about going back to classes. My schooling had ended in June 1939, and here we were in January 1941. After a break of over eighteen months, going back was a daunting prospect.

The day dawned and I—with polished shoes, clean shirt, smart coat and cap, gas mask over shoulder, and Mrs. Hooper at my side—was marched off to school.

Well, it was not exactly a school. It was an old disused church, occupied by teachers and pupils from Walthamstow. There was one big old church building, an old graveyard, and a few smaller outbuildings. Mrs. Hooper soon found the headmaster's office, which was located in one of the smaller structures.

"Take off your cap," ordered Mrs. Hooper. I ignored her.

We were soon standing before the desk of Mr. Taylor, the headmaster.

"Take off your cap," he ordered. I obeyed.

Mr. Taylor was a thin older white-haired man and clearly a master not to be trifled with. I tried to answer his questions carefully and respectfully.

"How old are you?" he asked.

"I shall be nine in April, sir," I answered.

"*Then you are eight now*," he forcefully reminded me.

It was the first five minutes of my first day at school in a year and a half, and already I had made a bad impression!

My teacher was to be Miss Cornu, whose class was held in yet another of the small outbuildings. She gave me an exercise book and a pen and told me to take care of them, as I would not get anymore. She told me where to sit, and I laboriously wrote my name on the book cover, taking care not to make any ink blots. Then I sat quietly and waited for morning playtime.

This was not at all like my old school. There, we formed lines in the assembly hall for morning prayers, before marching off to our classrooms.

"Swing those arms," the headmistress would order as the piano thundered "An English Country Garden" to four-four time.

Here, there was nowhere to assemble, and the old graveyard had to serve as playground.

Here at this school (which did not have a name), Tuesday mornings were for church. We had to form lines outside our buildings, to walk in one long column, to a nearby church for morning service. It was not much fun, but singing hymns was better than doing arithmetic. So with teachers in front and back, and on the side, the crocodile made its way from one old church to another.

My troubles started on the second or third day when Miss Cornu demanded to see my exercise book.

"What's this?" she asked, pointing to the book's empty pages.

I started to explain about being away from school for over a year and . . . Miss Cornu put her arm under mine.

"Pick up your things," she said and added, "I'm sorry to do this but . . ." With that, I was half carried, half guided to headmaster's study, where my demotion became official. I was to go down a class.

*   *   *   *   *

The main old church building was being used by two classes at the same time.

Big scholars sat in what had been the pews and faced what had been the altar. They occupied about two-thirds of the space.

Younger children, myself included, sat at school desks with their backs to the other class. Our teacher, a dark-haired young woman, must have felt cold most of the time, as "Miss" always wore an overcoat.

With lessons going on front and back, there was a temptation to swivel around to see what the other lot were doing. This was a mistake. Miss had a nasty habit of giving a hard slap to the back of any boy's head that might be facing the wrong direction. There was never a warning. The first sign of trouble was a sharp stinging pain followed by a vision of flashing lights.

She hit me only once, and from then on I carefully turned to face her whenever she came near, denying her the chance to strike! Her punishment list was lopsided, as some boys were often whacked, others not at all. One boy, the class dunce, was always being punished. No wonder he was a fool. I thought that she had probably knocked the sense out of him.

Girls were never punished.

* * * * *

Although all children at this school came from Walthamstow schools, I did not know or recognise any of them. Some had been in Rushden so long they spoke with Midland accents. I did not make friends with any of them. At playtimes, I would stand huddled, hands in pockets, trying to keep warm, while other kids chased around the old gravestones.

Once, the mayor of Walthamstow came to see us. We could tell he was important by the heavy gold chain of office that he wore around his neck. Mr. Taylor brought him to each class where he shook hands with the teacher, spoke individually with some of the children, and asked them questions like, "What did you have for dinner?" and "How are you getting on with your 'people'?"

He must have been satisfied with the answers, because I never saw him again.

*   *   *   *   *

Mother, and sometimes Dad, would come to visit us at weekends. They and the Hoopers would go out together to the Hoopers' own set of social clubs.

It came as a surprise, that day in early spring, when Mother arrived and announced we were going home. The air raids were not so bad now, and we could go back with her. She packed our things into a bag, ordered us to say our good-byes, and off we went, to the bus station, and home.

It was sad to leave. I really liked Mrs. Hooper and wished my behavior had been better.

That was the last time I saw the Hoopers, or Rushden.

CHAPTER XII

4 April 1941	Rommel's troops enter Benghazi.
5 April	Mussolini orders evacuation of Addis Ababa.
Early AM 6 April (Palm Sunday)	Germans bomb Belgrade. Seventeen thousand civilians die in one day. Yugoslav airfields are bombed, at the same time destroying most of its air force.
6 April	German army invades Yugoslavia.
6 April	German army invades Greece from Bulgaria.
6 April	Port of Piraeus is bombed. Eleven cargo ships and port installations are destroyed when the ammunitions ship Clan Fraser is hit.
6 April	RAF bombers based in Greece hit railway yards in Bulgaria.
8 April	Luftwaffe hits Coventry again.
PM 8 April	German army takes the Greek port of Salonica.
9 April	RAF bombs Berlin.
10 April	Italians surrender Eritrea to British forces.
10 April	Twenty-four thousand Australian and British troops are besieged at Tobruk as Rommel's German and Italian army advances eastward.
10 April	Germans capture Zagreb, and Croatia is declared an independent state.

13 April 1941	*German forces occupy Belgrade.*
16 April	*London is heavily bombed. Over two thousand civilians are killed.*
17 April	*Yugoslav government surrenders to Germans.*
18 April	*A British army brigade lands in Irak.*
24 April	*British, ANZAC,[25] and Polish troops in Greece start evacuating to Crete, abandoning tanks and heavy equipment.*
25 April	*British and ANZAC troops retreat from Thermopolae.*
26 April	*Rommell's army reaches Sollum, Egypt.*
28 April	*Irak seals British airbase at Habbaniya. Two thousand two hundred military and nine thousand civilians are trapped.*
5 May	*Emperor Haile Selassie reenters Addis Ababa exactly five years after Mussolini took it.*
May	*Russia gives diplomatic recognition to new pro-Nazi Iraki government.*
7 May	*Hull is bombed. Twenty-three German bombers are shot down.*
8 May	*Royal Navy capture German submarine U-110 in North Atlantic, along with its cipher books and Enigma code keys, as Sub Lieutenant Balme leads boarding party of eight from destroyer HMS Bulldog. Many experts say this is the most valuable prize the Royal Navy ever won. For many months, they could read all signals to U-boats in the Atlantic. U-110 commander Lt. Julius Lemp, who died in this action, was captain of U-30 that sank the Athenia, 3 September 1939.*
8 May	*German commerce raider Pinguin is sunk in Pacific by cruiser HMS Cornwall.*
8 May	*Heavy raids on Glasgow and Liverpool docks where thirteen merchant ships are sunk.*

---

[25] Australian and New Zealand Army Corps.

10 May 1941	*Hitler's deputy, Rudolf Hess, parachutes into Britain, saying he has come to make peace.*
10 May	*London is heavily bombed. House of Commons is destroyed. Nearly 1,500 civilians are killed in one night.*
13 May	*German aircraft established at base in Mosul, Irak.*
14 May	*Massive German/Italian air attacks against Malta costs them seventy-seven planes destroyed. RAF loses sixty fighters, many on the ground.*
15 May	*German aerial bombardment of Crete begins.*
18 May	*Troops of British-led Arab Legion relieve Habbaniya after three hundred-mile desert crossing from Transjordan.*
20 May	*After mass air raids, German airborne troops land in Crete and suffer heavy casualties (including three generals and five thousand men killed) to capture Maleme airfield and fly in reinforcements PM Twenty-first. Hitler refuses to allow his parachute troops into any further major actions. For the rest of the war, they fight as ordinary infantry.*
22 May	*In fight to stop landing barges reaching Crete, cruisers HMS Gloucester and Fiji and two destroyers are lost to massive air attacks. Battleships HMS Warspite and Valiant are damaged. One hundred and fifty German barges fail to reach Crete. Estimated four thousand German soldiers drown.*
23 May	*HMS Kelly, under Capt. Lord Louis Mountbatten, is lost to Stukas with 130 lives.*
24 May	*German battleships Bismarck and Prinz Eugen in action with battleships HMS Prince of Wales and HMS Hood in North Atlantic. Hood is lost with 1,500 men.*

24 May 1941	*Italian troopship* Conte Russo, *taking 1,500 reinforcements to Libya, is sunk by British submarine.*
25 May	*The king of Greece, who with his government had been evacuated to Crete, is evacuated again to Egypt.*
27 May	*Battleship* Bismarck *is sunk by British naval force, killing over two thousand Germans.*
27 May	*Following fierce fighting by ANZAC, British, and Greek forces, the Allied commander, New Zealand General Freyberg, orders evacuation of Crete.*
27 May	*Rommel's troops capture Helfaya Pass, back to where the Italians had been some months before.*
28 May-1 June	*Evacuation from Crete. Sixteen thousand five hundred Allied troops are brought to Egypt, and another one thousand men would be rescued clandestinely. In all, thirteen thousand Allied soldiers plus two thousand sailors are lost in the battle for Crete, as are three cruisers and six destroyers. While the Germans have lost over fifteen thousand men and two hundred planes.*
30 May	*Irak asks Britain for armistice.*
4 June	*Death, by natural causes, at age eighty-two of Kaiser Wilhelm II in Doorn, Holland.*
8 June	*British, Dominion, and Free French forces, entering Lebanon and Syria, are opposed by forty-five thousand strong Vichy French force under General Dentz. (In the British Palestine forces serves a young Moyshe Dayan.)*
15 June	*British Eighth Army fails in attack against Rommel's army at Libyan frontier.*
21 June	*Vichy French forces in Damascus surrender to British.*
AM 22 June	*Germany invades USSR exactly 129*

	years after Napoleon crossed the river Neman on his way to Moscow and defeat.
	One hundred and sixty-four divisions (about two million men) move east, supported by 2,700 warplanes.
22 June 1941	*Italy and Rumania declare war on USSR.*
26 June	*Germans capture city of Dvinsk.*
26 June	*Finland declares war on USSR.*
27 June	*Hungary declares war on USSR.*
28 June	*Soviets suffer over 300,000 soldiers killed or captured and 2,500 tanks destroyed, as area near Minsk falls to Germans.*
29 June	*"Scorched earth policy" is ordered by Stalin. All useable stores of food, fuel, machines, animals, buildings, everything to be destroyed by retreating Russians.*

Chapter XII Put That Light Out or A Woman's Work Is Never Done *April-June 1941*

> *Hitler changes his socks several times a day— because he smells defeat.*
>
> —Music hall joke

The Walthamstow to which we returned was not the old Walthamstow we left six months earlier. There had been so many changes.

For one thing, the shop windows had disappeared. Where once fashions, furniture, hats, and shoes were displayed, now only painted boards could be seen on shop fronts. In the centre of each board, a small pane of glass allowed passers-by to see what kind of establishment they were peering into. Still open for business of course, shopkeepers would not risk those valuable big heavy sheets of plate glass to enemy action. Some boarded, or lightly bomb-damaged, shops displayed printed stickers announcing "Business as Usual." The slogan seemed to be everywhere, and that too became a catch phrase.

In the blackout, with all shops in darkness, it was not possible to see if they were open or closed. For that reason, it became customary to have an illuminated sign in the window or door and the word "open" cut into cardboard and covered with tinted cellophane. It would be just visible in the darkness without breaking the blackout regulations.

All buses and trams had an antiblast wide woven cloth stuck to the inside of their windows. That meant passengers could not see out or look for a stop. London Transport solved the problem by cutting little six-inch square holes in the centre of these cloths; a sort of window in a window.

To add to our discomfort the interior bus lights were reduced to a dim twilight.

Barrage balloons were a novelty. Big silver silk bags with triple fins at the tails and tethered by steel cables to winches on the ground. Every park and green open space had its barrage balloon and RAF winch crew. The balloons flew as high as they would go on clear, still evenings, as a deterrent to German dive-bombers. Since no dive-bombers attacked us, I suppose they were successful. For that reason, I drew comfort from them, as did most people.

Granny Chapman was not so sure.

"They're full of gas, ain't they?" she asked.

"Then what if one falls on us, eh? *We'll all be gassed!*"[26]

Our mum agreed with her.

I knew there was something wrong with this idea, but just could not explain what! It was an idea to be expected of

---

[26] Barrage balloons were hydrogen filled.

Granny who refused to believe that Kitchener was really dead—and our mum agreed with that too.[27]

Searchlights would put on a nightly show of their own, as their bright beams swept the night sky for German bombers. Every now and again, they found one, and then all the beams would shine on to the one aeroplane, making big crisscross patterns in the sky. Once caught in their lights it must have been almost impossible to escape, and the bombers became targets for the ack-ack guns.

"They're Germans up there, ain't they, Mum?" I once asked. "In those aeroplanes, ain't they, Mum?"

"Yes," she answered sadly. "And they are some poor mothers' sons."

Grown-ups say funny things sometimes.

*   *   *   *   *

Fewer men came knocking at the front door. Well, the milkman, coalman, window cleaner, and insurance men still came, but so many of the prewar callers were missing.

The fruiterers, greengrocers, butchers, and bakers, with their horse-drawn carts, were nowhere seen. Neither were the boys, who, with bucket and shovel, came around selling horse manure. I am not sure about the rag-and-bone man; with the need for salvage, he suddenly became important. The irregular sellers like the muffin man, who carried his wares in circular trays on his head. Or the shrimp-and-winkle man who traded in pint pots from baskets atop his head; the chimney sweep, and the knife sharpener, all gone.

The man with the barrel organ was never a common sight

---

[27] National war hero Field Marshal Lord Kitchener was secretary for war when in 1916 he was lost at sea as the cruiser taking him to Russia struck a mine. It was Lord Kitchener's face and pointing finger on the famous recruiting poster "Kitchener Needs You."

around our way. He was more a regular in Granny Schofield's street.

The ice cream man—with his white coat, tricycle, and bell—had disappeared for sure. It was now illegal to make or sell ice cream, and there was no more "Stop me and buy one."[28]

I asked my mum why we had insurance men. "It's so you can be buried when you die," she explained. "If you didn't have insurance, you'd have to go on the 'nine o'clock trot.'"

"What's that?"

"A pauper's funeral," she went on.

"An unpolished, plain wooden coffin, only two mourners, and the cart comes at nine o'clock in the morning."

"Years ago, a lot of them made that ride." She stood and thought for a moment, no doubt about some of those people who had made the ride.

"Old Mrs. Mac's husband," she added sadly, "he went on the 'trot.'"

A funny thing about "insurance men"—we, children, were warned not to mention them in front of Father. Our dad did not believe in insurance.

Not only were the ranks of street vendors thinner, the in-house helpers had disappeared altogether.

The wild, overgrown state of our garden showed that the gardener was not coming around anymore. It used to be kept neat by old Mr. Fisher, whose services we shared with two other houses in the road. Mum told me Mr. Fisher now had a good job doing war work.

The woman who came to help with the washing—well, that was another story. It took at least a whole day to do a week's washing in our house.

"Washing don't get clean if you don't boil it," Granny insisted. So every piece of linen had to be dunked in the "copper" of boiling water, while she poked at it with a wooden paddle. I do not know why they called it a "copper." It was

---

[28] A prewar ice cream sales' slogan.

really a sort of iron cauldron with a built-in gas ring underneath.

From the boiling water to Mum or other washerwoman at the butler sink, where clothes were scrubbed and rinsed in clear water. Next step, the mangle, that cast iron piece of old machinery that lived just outside the back door. The mangle stood nearly five feet tall and supported two wood-covered cylinders, each about eighteen inches long by six in diameter. They were rotated by a series of black grease covered iron cogs that were themselves worked by a large hand-driven wheel. This whole wonderful contraption was used to squeeze most of the water out of the rinsed laundry. As a last step, everything was pegged on to the washing lines that ran the length of the garden. Well almost, but not quite everything went on the clothesline; Mother's and Granny's bloomers did not. They thought it unseemly to display certain garments in public!

No wonder the washing took a complete day. Longer if the weather was bad. And then there was ironing! Mother had several flatirons and at least two gas rings burned as she moved them around to keep the right temperature. The correct temperature for irons was measured by the 'spit test'!

Ironing was hard work according to our mum, and Granny could not help because of her paralysed hand.

Dad once brought home a new electric iron for Mother. She was suspicious, but agreed to try it. To her, anything electric was dangerous, and her fears were to be proved well founded. As she plugged the thing into its socket, there was a loud bang and sparks flew!

"Never again!" she screamed. "We'll all be bloody well killed," and with that, she threw Dad's new iron out onto the garden lawn. She refused, and could not be persuaded, to try again. The tradition of the old flatirons lived on at our house until well after the war.

But wait. The wash day did not end with ironing. Last but not least came the airing cupboard, that place with wooden slats for shelves, just above the hot water tank. Here neatly pressed linen was stacked and left to air, before being stored in chests of drawers.

Sprigs of lavender placed between layers of sheets, shirts, and underwear made the last step of this long and labourious procedure.

*   *   *   *   *

The number and intensity of air raids now was about the same as it had been before we left London. The difference was on the ground, as people seemed better prepared. Everyone knew where and how to take cover, what to do, and where to go in any kind of emergency. The civil defence services looked so much more competent and professional, too. ARP wardens were patrolling the streets every night, looking for blackout violations among other things.

"Put that light out" had become another catch phrase, and a sort of joke. Everybody was saying it to everybody else.

Static water tanks started to appear on cleared bomb lots. At some sites where buildings had been destroyed, the rubble was carted away and ribbed and flanged steel sheets bolted or welded together to make water storage tanks. They were for use of the fire engines in case the main hydrants should be put out of action.

These water tanks, about four or five feet high, at first open topped, until the boys started using them as swimming pools. Later on, other kids started throwing rubbish into the water, and the authorities fitted wire mesh on top of the containers.

Another new landscape feature was the appearance of double rows of solid blocks of steel-reinforced concrete. Each block was a four- or five-foot cube, and about four feet apart. These lines of tank traps stretched, like some modern day Hadrian's Wall, across roads and countryside. Just such a defence line stretched across Chingford Road near the

Crooked Billet. There was a break in the line in the middle of the road, just wide enough to let buses and lorries pass through. My dad had explained to me that the little concrete moveable covers in the road would be charged with antitank mines, if German tanks were about.

I would have to wait a year until my legs were long enough to climb on to the tank traps and play at jumping block to block—like the older boys did!

*   *   *   *   *

Our parents' circle of friends at the club and the Billet were still there. Well, most of them—although a number of their sons and young men family members had been called up for the forces.

One of the barmen at the Billet had been injured in putting sand on an incendiary bomb. That was just before Christmas. He was already back at work by the time I heard about it, so his wounds could not have been serious.

Our house, so far, had survived the blitz.

*   *   *   *   *

"Chapel End School 1914"

So read the name high on the outside wall. And the name was to remind us of the days, not long ago, when Chapel End was a hamlet in its own right, and not just a tiny sub section of the Borough of Walthamstow.

A former headmaster at Chapel End had been one Mr. Hilton, whose son was the famous author and Hollywood screenplay writer James Hilton. He penned such popular works as *Lost Horizon* and *Random Harvest*. His first successful novel, *Good-bye, Mr. Chips*, told the story of a schoolmaster's slow rise to headmaster. It is generally believed that old Mr. Hilton was the model for "Mr. Chips." If this is true, let me say, here and now, that Chapel End School did not, in any way whatsoever, resemble the Brookfield College of the novel!

The three-storey red brick building stood inside its own asphalt-surfaced playgrounds, inside an iron railing fence and gates.

Most public buildings, and private houses too, had lost, or were about to lose, their iron gates and railings to the scrap metal drive. The collectors did not ask permission. They just came around with oxyacetylene cutters and helped themselves. Schools must have been excused as special cases. Even the old, cemented over, tramlines had to be dug up for scrap. Although only three floors, Chapel End was a tall building, as each floor was about eighteen or twenty feet high.

I remembered the school playground from the day of that first evacuation. The day, nearly two years earlier, when we had waited for buses to take us to the train, to take us away to the country.

This was not the Chapel End of two years ago. The school was now open—well, most of it. Today, here in the junior school, which occupied the middle floor, Mr. Hall was headmaster. There was no doubt about that, and no one dared dispute his authority. Even some of the teachers appeared nervous when Mr. Hall addressed them. His dark steel gray three-piece suit matched his dark steel gray hair and thick moustache. I do not know if he owned only one suit or just wore the same kind of clothes all the time. I suspect the latter, as Mr. Hall was a gentleman of rigid tastes, habits, and opinions from his starched butterfly collar to his polished black boots.

He carried a cane in one hand most of the time. It was a blackboard pointer but had many other uses.

I was led into the first-year class of the junior school, where the only qualification for admission was to be the right age. One had to be between eight and nine. Many of the children who would normally be here were away, evacuated. Chapel End was open, but not full, so all the eight-year-olds—be they boys, girls,[29] scholars, or dunces—were all in together. Some of my new classmates like Robby Maitland and Clarence Snoad lived in our road.

Lucky for me, my little sister was in the infants' school, one floor down. A chap does not like to be encumbered by a girl, even if she is a relative!

There was a lot of movement among children, and teachers too. With new kids always being brought into the class, only to disappear again days or weeks later. Even teachers were not at all permanent, and new ones came and went.

One of the lady teachers who came and went was married! She was Mrs. Something. My mum told me that some married women were being accepted back as teachers because of the war.[30]

Schoolmasters called into the army were being replaced by women. Our mum said, "Women will be doing a lot of men's jobs before this war is over. Postmen, bus conductors, and factory workers, just like the last war." Our mum was to be proven right.

I saw Morse (the boy from that first evacuation to the country) one day in the hall. He was walking in one direction. I was walking in the opposite direction. We slowed our pace and turned to stare at each other as we passed by. Nothing was said.

Arthur Brewer was a ginger-haired little boy whose parents ran a greengrocer shop in Wood Street. He approached me one day in the playground with a proposition. For a shilling something, he could get me into the George Formby Fan Club! Yes, I agreed—it sounded like a good idea—and gave him my money the very next day. For the next few days, I hurried home from school to see if there was any post. Oh, the

---

[29]   Until the war, Chapel End Boys and Girls schools were completely separate.

[30]   Before the war, all women teachers were required to be unmarried.

excitement I felt when that official letter arrived with my name printed on the envelope. Inside was a signed glossy photograph of George Formby playing his ukulele banjo, a letter of welcome into the club, and a membership card with my official number. It all made me feel very special. From now on, when I went to the pictures for a Formby film, it would be as a real fan. Other kids in the audience would be just that, the audience. But I would be an official fan. George Formby knew who I was!

* * * * *

The news on the wireless was somehow different now. No weather forecasts were permitted, not on radio or in newspapers, but it was not just the content; the presentation had changed. Newsreaders would not only identify the station, but themselves, and became familiar names where once they had been anonymous.

"This is the BBC home service broadcasting from London on 'this' or 'that' meter band. Here is the news and this is Frank Phillips or Wilfred Pickles, or Alvar Lydel reading it."[31]

The fact that German radio was broadcasting propaganda in English and making it sound as if coming from British sources probably had something to do with the change.

Several German stations regularly broadcast propaganda, and the most famous speaker of all was jokingly referred to as "Lord Haw Haw." The stations broadcast popular music and propaganda speeches. Lord Haw Haw told us how sorry he was that we, British, had to suffer food shortages and bombing. We had lost the war anyway, and if we would surrender, the Germans would treat us well! We listened to him at home on our wireless set only once. He had a funny-sounding voice, and all the BBC and music hall comedians

---

[31] All newsreaders were men.

imitated or made jokes about him.[32] The real news was usually bad enough as it was. When the newsman said things like, "After heavy fighting, our forces withdrew to pre-prepared defence positions," even a nine-year-old knew what that meant!

Popular songs on the wireless had changed. "We're Going to Hang Out Our Washing on the Siegfried Line" was heard no more. They were singing "Oh, What a Surprise for the Duce"[33] as the Duce's army took a beating in Greece. Then the Germans came to his aid, the tide turned, and that song was not heard again.

We went to a live radio broadcast—Mum, little sister, and me. The programme was called *London Sings* and was broadcast by the BBC every week from a different London cinema.

This particular week was the turn of the Walthamstow Granada. Everyone coming into the cinema was given a song sheet with the words of popular and other songs. The MC/conductor up on the stage made us sing all the songs on the sheet. It took half an hour. Then the red "On the Air" sign went on and we had to sing the complete programme again, by which time everybody was sick of the whole business.

I think the purpose of this event was to let the rest of the country know that London was still alive and kicking—so to speak. I cannot remember if we enjoyed the picture.

*   *   *   *   *

---

[32] "Lord Haw Haw" was William Joyce, a former member of Mosley's Fascist Party and once a political candidate in Shoreditch. He was hanged for treason, London 1946. The old village stocks stood beside a churchyard in Lower Clapton Road, Hackney. A plaque explained their history. Some wags added another sign during the war. It read "Reserved for William Joyce."

[33] The Duce (pronounced *dook-shay*) was Benito Mussolini, the Italian dictator.

The conversation of the men at the clubhouse bar was as interesting as ever. For example, "By invading Russia, old Hitler just lost the war," so went the popular wisdom. He could never have won anyway, but this made his defeat a certainty.

The club women were lamenting the death of singing star Al Bowlly.[34]

*   *   *   *   *

My classmate and neighbour, Clarence Snoad, was not a particular friend of mine. I did not really like him, or his younger brother Damian, or their mother for that matter. I once had a fistfight with Damian. Although he was a year and a bit younger than me, we were about the same size. At first, we stood facing each other shouting insults. Then the words turned to punches as with clenched fists and straight arms we assailed each other with blows. This lasted for all of five seconds, when Damian ran away crying. His brother did not come to his aid.

Mrs. Snoad was a fat woman who did "a lot of gossiping and little housework," according to my mum. I once heard our mum telling Granny about her, "Never gets down to scrub her floors! No, uses a mop." Then they exchanged knowing expressions as if they both knew what kind of a woman that made her.

Mr. Snoad was a trader of some sort. He dealt in grease or coal tar or something, so at least he had an excuse for looking dirty. His wife and sons did not. They were a scruffy trio living in a scruffy house and using posh accents to talk about money and their family importance!

---

[34]   The popular radio and recording artiste, along with the "Snakehips" Johnson Dance Band, was among the more than two hundred staff and customers killed when a famous London cabaret took a direct hit.

"Oh yes," Mrs. Snoad once boasted to our mum, "old grandfather Snoad left a thousand pounds to each of his grandchildren when he died."

"A thousand pounds, huh?" our mum repeated after she had gone. "A thousand pounds of shit more like it!"

On another occasion, Mother had referred to the Snoad boys as, "A couple of sawn-off Burlington Berties."

*   *   *   *   *

The Maitlands were the very opposite of the Snoads.

While the Snoads boasted of their imagined wealth and influence, the Maitlands pleaded poverty. A thin little woman was Mrs. Maitland, whose Hamlet-style, straight grey hair was usually covered by a battered "pork pie" hat. She had the voice of someone about to burst into tears at any moment, almost crying as she talked of high prices in the shops, illnesses, deaths, and other miserable subjects. Two brown stains under her nose advertised her snuff-taking habit.

Mum was not taken in by her neighbour's tales of woe.

"Her husband's got a steady war factory job," she told me. "They are not as hard up as they pretend."

CHAPTER XIII

29 June 1941	*Evacuation of two hundred thousand children begins as Leningrad prepares for siege.*
29 June	*Ukrainian city of Lvov is taken by German forces.*
30 June	*HMAS* Waterhen[35] *is sunk by German dive-bombers off Libya.*
	In separate action cruiser HMAS Sydney *sinks Italian cruiser* Bartolomeo Colleoni.
1 July	*Germans enter Riga.*
2 July	*General Auchinleck is appointed commander in chief of Allied forces in the Middle East.*
3 July	*In a broadcast to the Soviet people, Stalin calls for formation of guerrilla groups behind enemy lines.*
7 July	7 July '41
	In a letter to Monsieur Stalin, Churchill promises to "do everything that time, geography, and our growing resources allow. The longer the war lasts, the more help we can give." He describes the daily heavy bombing raids on German industrial centres. "This will go on," he says. "Thus we hope to force Hitler to bring back some of his air

---

[35] His Majesty's Australian ship.

power to the West and gradually take
some of the strain off you."
His letter ends, "We have only to go on
fighting to beat the life out of these
villains."

10 July 1941   In a memo to First Sea Lord, Churchill
calls for all possible help for Russia: "A
premature peace by Russia would be a
terrible disappointment . . . These
people have shown themselves worth
backing, and we must make sacrifices."

12 July   Britain and USSR sign pact of "mutual
assistance." Both agree not to make a
separate peace.

About 14 July   Heavy RAF bombing of German cities.

21 July   Luftwaffe bombs Moscow for first time.

About 24 July   British force of aircraft carriers HMS
Furious and HMS Victorious, plus eight
cruisers and destroyers, sail for Arctic
as support for Russian supply lines.

About 26 July   Japanese forces, with Vichy French
approval, enter Saigon, French Indo-
China.

26 July   Italian "human torpedoes" fail in attack
on Valeta harbour.

27 July   Red Army suffers heavy losses as
Smolensk is surrounded.
Stalin orders execution of several Soviet
generals for their "failures."

30 July   German army report eight hundred
thousand prisoners taken and twelve
thousand tanks knocked out on Russian
front so far. Few of these Russian
prisoners would survive the war.

2 August   Red Army begins counterattack at
Yelnya. This will give them their first
victory of the war.

9-11 August   Churchill and Roosevelt confer aboard
HMS Prince of Wales off Newfoundland.

11 August   Soviet air force bombs Berlin for first time.

25 August   British and Indian troops enter Iran
from the south. Soviet forces enter and

	occupy the north as British and Soviet governments demand Iran accept their protection.
25 August 1941	British/Canadian/Norwegian forces land at Spitzbergen, destroy installations, evacuate civilians.
26 August	Germans take Dnepropetrovsk, Ukraine.
28 August	Russians suffer heavy casualties as they evacuate Tallinn by sea.
3 September	First gas chamber is used at Auschwitz, killing about eight hundred Russian POWs.
8 September	Finnish forces cut Leningrad Murmansk railway. Leningrad is besieged.
Autumn	Professors Harold C. Urey and GB Pegram of Columbia University, acting as emissaries of U.S. government, arrive in England. They meet British government scientists (MAUD committee) who are working on production of an atomic bomb. It is agreed to form a cooperative effort, and in 1943 a policy committee is established with United States, United Kingdom, and Canada. British and Canadian scientists go to USA where the bomb is to be built and tested.
10 September	Nazis execute trade union officials in Oslo.
19 September	German troops enter Kiev.
29 October	U.S. destroyer Reuben James is torpedoed and sunk by U-boat. One hundred and fifteen Americans die. United States takes no action.
30 October	In message to Stalin, FDR says he has approved $1,000,000,000 in Lend Lease to USSR. Interest-free repayments to begin five years after end of war.
31 October	Luftwaffe bombs Moscow.
7 November	RAF bombs Berlin and Ruhr.
7 November	Leningrad is heavily bombed by Luftwaffe.

8 November 1941	Eight German/Italian supply ships for North Africa are sunk by Royal Navy.
8 November	Germans reach town of Tichvin. Seventy-five miles east of Leningrad.
About 9 November	The Cetnik Command in Yugoslavia announces that Tito's Communists are bigger menace than Nazis and vows to fight both!
November	A report out of Leningrad puts starvation deaths at four hundred a day and rising.
14 November	Aircraft carrier HMS Ark Royal is lost in action off Gibraltar.
18 November	Eighth Army launches major offensive against German/Italian front in North Africa.
19 November	Off coast of W. Australia HMAS Sydney is sunk with all hands (645) in surprise attack by German commerce raider Kormoran, which sank a few hours later.
20 November	Germans take Rostov-on-Don.
25 November	Battleship HMS Barham is sunk in Mediterranean by U-boats. Eight hundred sixty are killed.
25 November	First gas chamber at Buchenwald is put to use under direction of Dr. Fritz Mennecke.
27 November	HMAS Paramatta is sunk by U-boats off Libya. One hundred and fifty are killed.
28 November	Germans are forced out of Rostov-on-Don.
	December begins in Russia with record cold temperatures.
1 December	German army fails in attempt to capture Moscow.
2 December	A British fleet led by battleship HMS Prince of Wales under Admiral Sir Tom Phillips arrives in Singapore.
5 December	Britain and the Dominions declare war on Finland, Hungary, and Rumania (who with Italy are allied with Hitler against USSR).

7/8 December 1941 [36]	*Japanese surprise attack on American, British, and Dutch bases in Pacific Ocean. Japanese fleet of six aircraft carriers with three hundred and sixty-six planes, two battleships, plus cruisers, destroyers, and submarines hit Honolulu. Eight U.S. battleships plus cruisers and other ships are destroyed or badly damaged. Two thousand three hundred and thirty Americans die.*
8 December	*Britain and USA declare war on Japan.*
8 December	*Japanese troops land Malay Peninsula from Siam.*
8 December	*Japanese planes bomb Hong Kong from China.*
8 December	*Japanese planes bomb Singapore and Dutch East Indies from French Indo-China.*
8 December	*First continuous executions using gas vans at Chelmno, Poland.*
9 December	*Japanese enter Bangkok.*
10 December	*Battleships HMS* Prince of Wales *and* Repulse *and over eight hundred men, including Admiral Phillips, are lost in mass attack by Japanese torpedo bombers*
10 December	*Japanese troops begin landing in Philippines.*
11 December	*Germany and Italy declare war on USA.*
11 December	*In landing attempt at Wake Island, two destroyers are sunk with loss of over a thousand Japanese.*
12 December	*Six hundred civilians die as Japanese bomb Penang.*
16 December	*Russians recapture Kalinin.*
16 December	*Japanese land at Sarawak.*
18 December	*Japanese land at Hong Kong from China.*

[36] American and British bases in Pacific are either side of the International Date Line.

19 December 1941	*Battleships HMS* Queen Elizabeth *and* Valiant *are damaged by Italian human torpedoes in Alexandria harbour.*
19 December	*In minefield off Tripoli, cruiser HMS* Neptune *is lost with over seven hundred men. Two other cruisers and a destroyer are badly damaged.*
20 December	*Japanese land at Mindanao, Philippines.*
25 December	*Eleven-thousand-strong British garrison at Hong Kong surrenders.*
26 December	*General MacArthur sets up HQ on island of Corregidor.*
27 December	*After abandoning Manila, MacArthur orders U.S. forces to retreat to Bataan.*
1 January 1942	*Meeting in Washington, Churchill, FDR, and twenty-four other signatories, including USSR, form the United Nations.*
2 January	*Japanese enter Manila.*
7 January	*Russians inflict heavy casualties on Germans at Novgorod.*
7 January	*In German offensive in Yugoslavia, Tito's partisans suffer heavy losses.*
About 10 January	*Japanese enter Port Swettenham and Kuala Lumpur, as British forces fall back on Singapore.*
17 January	*Destroyer HMS* Matabele *lost in Arctic action. Two hundred and fifty die.*
20 January	*Wannsee Conference of key German officials called by Reinhard Heydrich. They work out details for extermination of all non-Arayans in Europe. Adolf Eichmann is appointed chief of operations.*
21 January	*Rommel's Africa Corps advance on Benghazi as Eighth Army retreats. Tobruk falls.*
22 January	*General MacArthur orders retreat at Bataan.*
23 January	*Russians retake Kholm.*
26 January	*Irish Prime Minister de Valera protests*

	landing of U.S. troops in Northern Ireland.
29 January 1942	Russia and Britain sign Treaty of Alliance with Iran opening supply route to Russia.
31 January	Report from Leningrad that two hundred thousand die of starvation since siege began.
31 January	Last British troops in Malaya evacuate to Singapore island.
5 February	First British mission parachutes into Yugoslavia to liaise with Tito's partisans.
8 February	After heavy bombardment, Japanese troops land on Singapore island.
11-12 February	Three German battleships break British blockade of Brest.
14 February	Japanese parachute troops land in Sumatra.
15 February	Singapore surrenders to Japanese. Of the eighty-five thousand Malay, Indian, British, and ANZAC troops who surrender, about half would live to see war's end.
19 February	Japs bomb Darwin, Australia, and sink seventeen ships including a U.S. destroyer.
20 February	Philippine President Quezon leaves for Australia en route to USA.
23 February	Allied HQ Java moves to Australia.
23 February	British submarine torpedoes and damages battlecruiser Prinz Eugen.
26 February	USS Langley, America's first carrier, sinks with all thirty-two of its aircraft after Jap air attack south of Java.
27 February	Battle of Java Sea. A failed attempt to block Jap invasion of Java by a fleet (ABDA) of five cruisers (two Dutch, one British, one American, one Australian) plus nine destroyers (four American, three British, two Dutch, and no air cover) commanded by Dutch Admiral

	Doorman facing much bigger Jap fleet (including six carriers). Early in action two Dutch cruisers and three destroyers—HMS Electra, HMS Jupiter, HMNS Kortenaer—are lost. Admiral Doorman is killed.
28 February 1942	Steaming away from lost battle, cruisers USS Houston and HMAS Perth are sunk.
1 March	The damaged heavy cruiser HMS Exeter (veteran of Rio Plata), and the destroyers HMS Encounter and USS Pope serving as escorts, en route to Ceylon from Java Sea, are overtaken by Jap force in Indian Ocean. All three ships lost. Japs lose only two transports in entire encounter.
1 March	German internal report (General Halder) their own losses on the Russian front so far as two hundred thousand dead, eight hundred thousand wounded, four hundred thousand taken prisoner.
3 March	RAF bombs Renault factory at Billancourt.
5 March	Dutch authorities announce evacuation of Batavia, Java.

Chapter XIII Up the ARP, or Down with Skool
June 1941-March 1942

Q: How does an Italian admiral inspect his fleet?
A: In a diving suit.

—Playground joke

I think it was a Sunday morning when a taxicab carrying Bob Knight drew up to our front garden gate. He was the governor of the Goldsmiths Arms public house in Shoreditch, and a good friend of the family.

It was early morning. We were still wearing pyjamas and having breakfast when the knock on the door came. He brought the bad news that Granny's house had been bombed. Granny was not hurt because she regularly slept in the public air raid shelter. So did Aunt Ginnie, Uncle Wally, and their boys.

Dad dressed quickly and went off in the taxicab with his friend, back to Shoreditch, to help Granny.

Later that week, we went to visit what was left of Maidstone Street, and Granny Schofield's house. A big piece of the street and the next one had been blown away. The houses next to the hole in the ground were so badly damaged that Dad said they would have to be demolished. We could not get too close because of the police cordon stopping anyone going in or out.

Granny was safe enough and staying with another of her daughters. Her upright piano was safe too—although scratched and dirty, they said it could still be played! I think Uncle Alf had something to do with its salvage.

The Goldsmiths Arms was undamaged.

*   *   *   *   *

They gave a going-away party for the Lovegroves. The regular customers at the Billet clubbed together for a present. On their last night at the pub, and after the doors were shut, the customers had a little party and gave them the gift. I cannot remember what the gift was, but someone made a speech and presented it. I have forgotten who.

Since the bar was closed, my little sister and I attended. We, the only children present, sat quietly watching. It was sad to see them leave, but it was not as though they were going far. Mr. and Mrs. Lovegrove had taken a pub in Chingford, only a four-penny bus ride away!

*   *   *   *   *

After May of 1941, the air raids became fewer and less intense. Some people said we should thank Russia, meaning Hitler needed all his planes there, instead of here. Others thought Hitler had given up bombing us because of the heavy beating we had given him.

Just the same I was so proud—oh, so proud—when our dad joined the ARP and became an air raid warden. He went on a training course and came back a real qualified warden, tin hat and all. Dad showed me the instruction manual and explained what he had learned about saving lives and first aid and everything.

We went on the bus to Hackney to see Dad on patrol. He joined the Hackney, rather than Walthamstow ARP, to be nearer his business.

My mum, little sister, and I saw him at a street corner. It was almost his going off duty time and we had come to meet him, so we could all go out somewhere that evening. I stood with him for a little while, paced up and down with my hands behind my back, and sort of pretended that I, too, was a duty warden.

Dad had not complained when he was required to register. He did complain when he was called to take a medical examination for military service.

"Waste of time," he called it. "With my bad stomach and state of health . . . a waste of time."

*   *   *   *   *

Granny Chapman was a lot happier now that we were all at home again. She could, as she put it, "sleep in me own bed." And have her glass of ale before she went there too. Every evening, one of us would have to go to get Granny's pint of ale from the "Jug and Bottle." That's what she called the "off licence," and we kids called the "beer shop." Sometimes I went. Sometimes Mum went herself, and sometimes she sent Robby Maitland. He always got a penny for going. It was nice when Granny invited me to have a drink with her. She would pour some of her ale into an eggcup and let me sit with her. Only a little drop of beer for me. "'Cause it stops your growth," she said.

"I'm going to drink lots of beer when I grow up, Gran," I told her.

"Yes," she nodded sagely. "I'm sure you will."

Granny might have been happier, but her health was no better. She was often tired and forgetful, and she was burning more kettles and saucepans. She would "put the kettle on," and forget!

*   *   *   *   *

They introduced school dinners this year. For a small weekly sum, each child could be served a two-course hot dinner at midday every school day. I badly wanted to have dinner at school, but Mum said no. Since she and Granny were at home all day, that was where I must eat. It was a serious disappointment. Most of the other kids stayed, even Robby, who was a reluctant diner at first. He told us how he was sent for school dinners before the war, how they had been herded into the back of an open lorry and taken somewhere to be given stew and bread, and milk to drink. All the other kids were dirty and rough, and it was not a nice experience at all.

Our mum explained that was free food for the poor, and this was going to be very different. She was right, of course.

Gas mask drills were fun, but little else amused us. Apart from dinners, there was not much that I liked or wanted from school, although we did have interesting visitors from time to time. Usually a police, or civil defence officer, who would warn us about this or that danger. One speaker showed pictures and told us about antipersonnel bombs and booby traps that were being dropped by enemy planes. He stressed the dangers and warned us not to touch, but report anything suspicious.

Right after school, that same day, all the boys were out looking for booby traps and unexploded bombs to explode! Apart from these entertaining distractions, I just lived from bell to bell. Well, not exactly. The ringing of bells was now forbidden, both church and school variety. Ringing bells was the signal for *invasion*! Instead of the handbell, a prefect with a battered old bugle would go into the playground and blow with all his might! That was our call to classes. But the only class that really interested me was Mr. Ling's history lessons. Mr. Ling was not a form master, but went from class to class. He was a young man who wore his brilliantine-covered dark wavy hair brushed straight back. Unlike Mr. Hall, he owned several suits and ties in various styles and colours.

Mr. Ling, the history master, told us tales of knights in armour, and tournaments, and battles glorious. He would make his stories continuous, not hesitating to leave us with a "cliffhanger."

"And next time, I shall tell you how the battle ended."

"But, sir, please, sir," the boys would half plead, half demand, and all to no avail. Mr. Ling knew how to keep his class attentive. All the boys liked Mr. Ling.

Classes were mixed, of course. That meant boys and girls all together in the same class, but only the boys got excited about Mr. Ling's lessons. Girls sat quietly waiting for the time to pass.

It was this teacher who started my interest in stamp collecting. Most of the boys in my grade were keen on the hobby, and I persuaded my parents to buy me an album and some stamps to get started.

Packets of foreign stamps were on sale in toy shops and stationers for young collectors like me. A great number of the stamps, Free French Colonials, printed in England as a sort of unsubtle war propaganda.

At the same time, my parents gave a similar album and stamps to my little sister and ordered me to help her sort and mount them. This I did, but not with entirely honest motives. Knowing that girls did not appreciate stamps, I carefully helped her, reasoning that when she lost interest, her collection would come to me. I was right; she did, and it did.

*   *   *   *   *

Once upon a time, not long ago nor far away, there was a magic place. A land where all heroes were handsome, and beautiful heroines had that Max Factor look. Where there was no bad language nor excessive violence, and the gooders always beat the baddies in the end. A world where no one ever went to the lavatory, and all married couples slept in twin beds. A world anyone could enter for the price of a cinema ticket. A place that, today, is hard to find.

Walthamstow's finest picture palace was the Granada, an impressive building in the style of the Alhambra in Spain, so Mr. Ling told us. The Granada stood in Hoe Street near the top of High Street right in the centre of town, and near the best shops. It was a swanky place indeed, where the usherettes wore blue uniforms with pillbox hats and blue and gold capes. One of those girls had a nice singing voice. They would lead her on stage to perform for the restless audience whenever the projector broke down—which was often.

The smartly uniformed, military-looking doorman used to stand in a blaze of light at the plate glass doors, directing people to the ticket office, or upstairs tea rooms. Now, with the war and blackout, he stood in semidarkness with an electric torch, guiding people up and down the front steps.

The Granada had a beautiful big electric organ that could rise and fall from the orchestra pit. Between films, the organist would rise up with it to play popular songs, and the audience sang along to the words displayed on the screen. Picture shows at the Granada, and everywhere else, were always continuous. That means you go in at anytime, and go out when you reach the point at which you started!

The appearance of the organ used to be a good moment to get ice cream, sweets, or chocolate, but this was wartime, and we had to settle for cough drops or an apple. Our mum would not let us eat an apple while the house lights were down.

"In the dark, you can't see if there are any worms," she said.

*   *   *   *   *

They announced a dance in aid of prisoners of war to be held at the club, and posters went up naming the date. I had never been to a real dance before. Well, not with a professional dance band and expensive admissions tickets. This was to be a swell affair, with refreshments, door prizes, spot prizes, and everything.

The vicar of St. John's Church organised the committee for families of POWs. Mr. and Mrs. Hayward, who were club and pub friends of our parents, had a son in German prisoner-of-war camp. Mrs. Hayward was on that committee, and I think that is how the dance got to the club.

On the night of the dance, I wore my best suit, and my sister her newest frock. Mum and Dad were always well dressed, of course, although they were not really dancers. Dad would manage a shuffle around the floor for a slow waltz, but that would be about his limit. We, children, could not really dance, but would not let that interfere with our evening's entertainment.

The only dances I knew were the Palais Glide, the Lambeth Walk, and Knees Up Mother Brown!

Oh, the excitement! The billiard and card tables had been removed, the dart boards covered, and the main hall decorated with flags and bunting. Everybody was looking their best, with the girls in dance frocks and silver shoes, the young men not in uniform, in their best suits.

The dance band was not exactly like Jack Payne or Billy

Cotton. But they were lively and tuneful, and even had a crooner whose face was practically hidden behind a large microphone.

My little sister and I went behind the bar to get drinks for ourselves. We had to go behind because the bar was too high for us to be seen from the front. We waited patiently to catch the eye of the barman. Mr. Clark was not a full-time barman, but the groundsman who cut the grass and painted white lines on the sports pitches. Some evenings he helped inside the clubhouse. He came over to us, smiled, and asked, "Yes, young man? Yes, young lady?"

"Two gin and limes please," my little sister ordered.

For a six-year-old, she spoke with assurance, self-confidence, and near-perfect diction.

"Yes, miss," he answered.

Mr. Clark understood the game of pretend as played by children. He was a family man himself, although his children were now grown-up, and his two sons in the army. He returned with two glasses of lime cordial.

"Tuppence please," and after "Thank you" and "Come again," we took the drinks to our vantage point at the side of the hall. A place from which the whole dance floor was visible, but we were not. At the end of each piece of music, the dancers stopped, stood, and applauded. We, two little ones, clapped our encouragement along with everyone else. We were soon joined by other children of the club in their best outfits, and we watched, enthralled as couples danced by to the rhythm of the band. Mother brought us goodies to eat from time to time. We saw prizes given away, and we had more "gin and lime."

We were both sleepy by the time Mum and Dad said we were leaving. The dancers were not—sleepy, I mean. The band was still playing and the couples still dancing as we left to walk home.

We heard a few days later that the dance had been a big financial success.

CHAPTER XIV

7 March 1942	British General Alexander orders evacuation of Rangoon, Burma.
8 March	In Java, one hundred thousand American, Australian, British, Dutch, and Dutch East Indies forces surrender to Japs.
8 March	RAF starts new major offensive by bombing Ruhr.
10 March	Japs land Solomon Islands.
11 March	U.S. General MacArthur abandons Luzon and the Philippines for Australia.
14 March	Death camp opens at Belzec, in Poland.
23 March	Japs occupy British Andaman Islands in Bay of Bengal.
28 March	British commandos destroy dry docks at St. Nazaire, closing the Atlantic port to German battleships.
28 March	Heavy RAF raid on German Baltic ports.
1 April	Ten Norwegian merchant ships break out of a Swedish port. Only two reach Britain.
1 April	Twenty-three Allied merchant ships are sunk in Bay of Bengal.
5 April	Eight o'clock in the morning, Easter Sunday. Dive-bombers from Admiral Nagumo's fleet of Pearl Harbour veterans of five carriers, four battleships, three cruisers, eight destroyers attack harbour at Colombo,

	Ceylon. Destroyer HMS Tenedos plus armed merchantman Hector are sunk. Later, at sea, cruisers HMS Dorsetshire and Cornwall are lost.
6 April 1942	*Japs land on Admiralty Islands.*
6 April	*Japs bomb eastern coastal towns in India.*
7 April	*At Sobibor, Poland, a new death camp opens.*
9 April	*Surrender of U.S. forces on Bataan and Death March begins. Six thousand of seventy-five thousand American and Filipino POWs die of beatings, bayonets, starvation, and disease as they are force-marched into captivity.*
9 April	*One hundred and twenty-nine Jap-carrier-based planes attack Trincomalee harbour, Ceylon. Of the eleven RAF Hurricanes defending (the entire fighter force), nine are lost. Thirty-six Jap planes shot down. Off Trincomalee light carrier HMS Hermes (without aircraft) plus destroyer HMS Vampire are lost to Jap air attack.*
11 April	*British commandos destroy German tanker in Bordeaux harbour.*
13 April	*Japs bomb Mandalay, Burma. Two thousand civilians are killed.*
17 April	*Twelve RAF heavy bombers fly in daylight at rooftop level to hit engineering factory at Augsburg.*
18 April	*Tokyo bombed by sixteen-carrier-launched from USS Hornet—USAAF B25s under Lieutenant Colonel Doolittle. (It was not, at the time, made known "how" the B25s reached Tokyo!)*
21 April	*First German "underwater" tanker sails to supply U-boats on western side of North Atlantic.*
23-28 April	*Luftwaffe heavy bombing of British "cultural" centres, including Exeter, Bath, York, and Norwich, destroying*

	many historic buildings and landmarks. About 950 civilians die.
	"There is no other way to bring the English to their senses," said Dr. Goebbels.
27 April 1942	RAF bombs Baltic city of Rostock.
29 April	Japs take Lashio, China. Closing the Burma Road.
5 May	A British fleet led by battleship HMS Ramillies *plus carrier HMS* Illustrious *land troops and take port of Diego Suarez, Madagascar, against stiff resistance from Vichy French garrison. Aim is to deny Japs use as submarine base.*
6 May	American island fortress of Corregidor in Manila Bay surrenders to Japs.
7 May	Chief Justice of Philippines Jose Abad Santos is executed. He refuses to collaborate with Japs.
2-10 May	Battle of the Coral Sea marks the end of Jap advances south as invasion fleet heads for Port Moresby. About one hundred warplanes are destroyed (fifty-fifty United States/Japan) in history's first 100 percent navy air battle. U.S. carrier Lexington *and Jap carrier* Sheho *are sunk.*
8 May	German General Manstein opens summer offensive against Sevastopol.
9 May	Two aircraft carriers HMS Eagle *plus* USS Wasp *deliver 126 fighters to Malta virtually breaking the aerial siege.*
26-28 May	General Rommel's German/Italian army offensive in Libya is halted by General Auchinleck's British, Dominion, and Free French forces.
30-31 May	First RAF one-thousand-bomber raid hits Cologne.
31 May	Two Jap midget subs sink Australian depot ship Kuttabul *in Sydney harbour. Both subs are destroyed.*

31 May 1942	*Suicide attack by Jap midget subs sink British merchant ship and damage battleship HMS Ramillies in harbour at Diego Suarez, Madagascar.*
4 June	*Death of governor in Prague, Reinhard Heydrich (The Hangman), a week after bomb thrown at the thirty-eight-year-old Nazi fanatic and Hitler favourite's car. Almost two thousand Czech civilians are murdered as reprisals. The village of Lidice is bulldozed; all its men are shot, its women and children sent to concentration camps.*

Chapter XIV Don't You Know There's a War On? or That's Show Business *March-June 1942*

My landlady served sausages for breakfast this morning, but I didn't know what to spread on them: mustard or marmalade!
—Gillie Potter, BBC Radio Comedian

Oh, what a shock! The family was so surprised when a government letter arrived to say our dad was A1! Fit for military service. He stood silent for some time, thinking about it very carefully.

"Of course, just because I've passed the medical doesn't necessarily mean that I'll be called," he said and added, "After all, I am forty-two and done my share in 1918."

After some meditation, he went on, "It's nice to know that you're fit."

The letter meant that he could be called up; not that he definitely would be.

* * * * *

New people had taken over at the Crooked Billet. Dick and May Edge were now the governor and missus. Of Mr.

Edge, I heard people say he was from Ireland, and that he was "stage struck." Well, he looked all right to me—a polite, well-spoken, smartly dressed gentleman.

Mrs. Edge was a good-looking blond young woman, who had once been a professional actress and dancer.

In no time at all, they were accepted into, and became the centre of, the social group, built around the pub and club.

The news, as discussed by the men standing around the club bar, was still instructive. The big news event was Japan's entry into the war, but nobody knew much about the Japanese.

"On our side in the last one, weren't they?" someone asked. The men did not seem sure. None of their number served in the Far East.

"What about our Yankee cousins?" someone asked of nobody in particular, "Are they any good?" The consensus was that whilst all of these men had seen action in France in the last war, none could remember actually seeing an American! So ended that line of conversation and conjecture.

For the women, "shortages" was high on their list of worries. Shortages of silk stockings, of tea, eggs, number 8 batteries[37]—you name it, and it was hard to get! Topping their worry list was when the news said that the German army was only eighteen miles from the Russian capital.

*   *   *   *   *

On learning of Japan's attacks against us, I took immediate action. Rummaging through my toys, I found only one plaything marked "Made in Japan." It was a very small tin boat. I ran into the garden, put the toy on the concrete path, stamped and flattened it with the heel of my

---

[37]   Popular size torch batteries.

shoe. The remaining bits of metal I threw into the fire. That taught them a lesson!

*   *   *   *   *

Life under the authoritative régime at Chapel End was as miserable as ever. Mr. Hall had a passion for teaching us new hymns. We had to learn the words by heart because there were no hymn books, and verses were written on a blackboard set up on the assembly hall dais.

"We are but little children weak, nor born in any high estate . . . ," so went the first lines of his latest effort. What a degrading verse. I was determined not to sing. Many of my schoolmates must have been of the same mind, for most of the sound was coming from the piano, not the singers. The longer this dragged on, the softer our voices became.

Mr. Hall was furious. He forcefully threw his cane to the floor and, bending his head to child level, walked along the lines of standing nonsinging children. As he passed me, I sang, and when he had gone by, I stopped singing and just moved my mouth. It seems most of the others did the same thing, because Mr. Hall gave up.

"To your classrooms!" he ordered. "And arithmetic!"

*   *   *   *   *

It was about this time that National Savings Stamps and Certificates were introduced to us at school. It was explained to our class by the new young form mistress. The stamps would be on sale in one-penny, three-penny, six-penny, one-shilling, and half-crown denominations. Each value stamp would be a different colour. That, we could all visualise and understand. These adhesive-backed stamps could be saved by sticking them into a special book. When we had fifteen shillings saved (an unimaginable large sum of money), we could exchange them for one Savings Certificate. If we saved that Certificate for seven—or was it ten?—or some other unimaginable number of years, it could be cashed for an even bigger sum of money.

The teacher described it all enthusiastically, but I, for one, was not impressed.

"What if you don't get your money back?" I whispered to the girl sitting beside me.

"Please, miss, what if you don't get your money back?" she straight away asked the teacher.

The young woman looked flabbergasted!

"Who told you to say that?" she demanded to know.

"Please, miss, it was George Schofield."

"STAND UP, GEORGE SCHOFIELD!" the teacher screamed. "HOW DARE YOU . . . ," and on and on she went. I do not know why she made such a fuss. After all, I only asked.

Most schools, offices, and factories had National Savings Groups with targets, and the target was usually a Spitfire. A big drawing of a thermometer, or wall chart, indicated how much the group had saved, until it reached the purchase price of a Spitfire.

The junior school, however, did not have a Spitfire Fund. We were saving for an ambulance.

"It's just as important, you know," Mr. Hall would remind us. Well, that might have been true, but I still wished we had been saving up for a Spitfire.

*   *   *   *   *

It was true what they said about Mr. Edge, the new governor of the Billet. The bit about being stage struck, that is. In no time he became a shareholder in the Walthamstow Palace. Our dad was invited, along with some others, to be a shareholder in the theatre, too. I was so excited when he came home and told us about it, but my dreams of show business were soon to be shattered.

"The Palace is a dead house," proclaimed our dad, as he

sat at the dining table. "Always was and always will be 'cause it's in the wrong place," he went on.

He was right, I supposed. The building was nice enough, with twin towers in the Byzantine architectural style. (That is what Mr. Ling told us.) The seats were comfortable enough, and sometimes there was a good show, but it was a long walk to the nearest bus or train. At night, when the market shops and stalls were closed, High Street Walthamstow could be a dark and lonely place. Even so, we were regulars at this variety theatre, and Dad would always stop to speak with Mr. Loss, the manager.

The trouble with taking children to the variety theatre too often is their tendency to believe and copy whatever they see! Now, snatching the tablecloth from under the cups, cruet and cutlery, was a failed trick, but nothing was broken. I had seen a stage magician do it and tried to do the same. No harm done; Mother did not find out.

Another trick was not so safe, and could have turned tragic. On stage it looked easy as the be-feathered Red Indian chief threw knives at a girl standing before a board at the other side of the stage. Each knife thrown landed close to, but just missing, the scantily dressed young lady.

Next day, I persuaded my little sister, to stand still with her back to a door. She must have been about three at the time, so I would have been six, then with a set of Dad's sharp, pointed darts . . .

The first and second shots hit the door—then trouble. The sharp tip of the third dart caught her in the scalp! I rushed toward her and pulled the thing out. Tears came to her eyes as I patted her shoulder and pleaded, "Now don't say anything to Mum!"

She never did mention it to anyone. Well, nobody ever took me to task for the incident.

On another occasion, another magician had another trick. He held a piece of rope between outstretched hands, then folded it exactly in the middle. With a pair of scissors, he cut the rope in half and made a ball of it in his cupped hands.

After uttering the magic word, he pulled out the cord to show that it was one long piece again. "A magic rope," he said as he threw the cord out to the audience. We were sitting centre stalls near the front, and our dad raised his hand and caught the piece of rope.

"It's not really magic, is it?" I quietly asked Dad.

"No," he answered me, "Just a trick," and then it was all forgotten until later next day, when Dad produced the "magic" rope from his pocket.

"Let's see now," he mused as he stretched out the cord, folded it at the centre, and cut it with the scissors. He gathered the whole rope into a ball, said the magic word, and—*voila!*—the rope was back in one long length!

"It's true, it *is* magic!" I shouted in amazement.

"It really *is* magic," I repeated as Mum and Dad laughed.

Taking the magic rope, I did exactly as the stage magician and our dad had done. Folded it in the middle, cut with scissors, magic word, everything the same, but. As I pulled the string at both ends, I was left holding two pieces of rope! Our mum and dad did laugh.

It was Mother who explained it to me. "That magician might have been quick with the sleight of hand, but not quick enough for your father. He saw how it was done!"

Dad taught me how to perform that illusion.

*   *   *   *   *

I can think of at least one occasion when we, four Schofields, were the only people in the front stalls for a "first house" midweek. Friday and Saturday nights were well attended whatever the show, and Mondays saw a fair turnout because that was the free-ticket holders' night, when the shopkeepers, who displayed advertising, came en masse! Otherwise, a full theatre at the Walthamstow Palace was a rare event, and the "house full" board collected dust behind the ticket office.

It was about this time when we went to a midweek show with Mr. and Mrs. Vinson. The Vinsons managed the club, and appearing this week at the Palace was an old friend of theirs. Years before, Mr. Vinson had employed this star comedian in the club he ran.

I think the man's name was Billy "Something," and as was usual in these revues, the lead comedian ran the show. Meaning he employed all the other cast members.

After the "first house," my mum and dad, little sister and me, went backstage with the Vinsons to meet the star. It was all I expected, and more.

Through the dim lights and apparent confusion of the world behind the safety curtain, to the star's dressing room, it was nice to find that this star was the same off stage as on, when he joked and laughed his way through a costume change.

"If you are going to change, we can all wait outside the door," said Mrs. Vinson shyly. But he was out of one suit and into another before she could get up from her chair!

The grown-ups talked about old times for a little while, before they arranged to meet for a drink after the "second house."

Then we, children, were taken home. Perhaps Mum and Dad had forgotten, but this was not my first visit backstage at the Palace. I had been there before.

It happened like this. Just before the war when I was about six years of age, the Palace used to have "Carnaval Night" once a week. On a first house midweek, I think. There were games and prizes to be won.

On this particular evening, the compère, on stage, shone a light along the faces of people sitting in the audience, until the music stopped. Whoever was in the light beam at that moment was a winner, and this time it was me!

"The little boy in the white hat," announced the compère. And an usherette came and took me by the hand to lead the way up the steps beside the orchestra pit. On to the centre of the stage, where the prize of a large brightly colored rubber ball was presented.

"Given by 'such and such' toy shop of Walthamstow," the man was saying as the audience applauded.

The uniformed usherette led me by the backstage route to rejoin my parents. Past the long-legged chorus girls standing in the wings.

"Hello, little boy," one of them greeted me as I walked by, jealously clutching my new toy. Another quietly said something else, and they all laughed. They seemed such nice friendly ladies.

Back in the stalls and again seated between my parents, Dad's first question sounded strange. "Did you see the girls?" he whispered.

CHAPTER XV

4 June 1942	*Battle of Midway. Attempt by Japs to capture Midway Islands by Admiral Nagumo's fleet of eighty-plus ships, including four carriers. (U.S. Admiral Fletcher's smaller force of three carriers, including the hastily repaired* Yorktown, *had the advantage of knowing Japs "secret" codes.) In a long confused battle, all four Jap carriers plus their three hundred planes are lost. Admiral Fletcher loses the* Yorktown, *a destroyer, and 150 planes. Experts agree, this defeat marks the beginning of the end for Japan.*
21 June	*Tobruk falls to Rommel as South African General Klopper surrenders his thirty-thousand-man garrison.*
23 June	*First group of Polish mental asylum inmates is sent to Auschwitz.*
July	*Treblinka II death camp opens.*
3 July	*Last fort at Sevastapol falls to Germans.*
21 July	*A Jap infantry division (fifteen thousand men) lands New Guinea coast north of Port Moresby. Outnumbered Australians retreat across Owen Stanley Mountains.*
7 August	*Sixteen thousand U.S. Marines land Guadalcanal in Solomon Islands. Three U.S. cruisers are lost in this battle.*

7 August 1942	*Emil Klaus Fuchs, German refugee, becomes naturalized British citizen and swears allegiance to his new country, where he is working (University of Birmingham) on development of atomic bomb. (In 1950, he will be sent to prison for fourteen years as a Soviet spy.)*
9 August	*Cruiser HMAS Canberra is lost in same action near Guadalcanal as Jap cruiser Kako.*
10 August	*A British naval force in desperate attempt to get supplies to Malta suffers heavy losses from German/Italian planes and submarines. Carrier HMS Eagle plus destroyer HMS Foresight plus five loaded cargo ships are sunk. Five cargo ships reach Malta. Returning to Gibraltar, the cruisers HMS Manchester and HMS Cairo are lost.*
19 August	*Operation Jubilee. Combined operations raid on Dieppe. Of the five thousand Canadian, one thousand British, fifty American, and twenty-five Free French soldiers sent ashore. One thousand are killed; two thousand are taken prisoner. The German defenders lose three hundred and forty-five killed, four taken prisoner. Forty-five Luftwaffe planes are downed. To those involved—a futile waste of lives. To most experts later—a valuable lesson for D day.*
19 August	*German Swastika raised on Mount Ebrus (18,500 feet), highest of the Caucasian mountains.*
24 August	*En route Guadalcanal Jap carrier Ryuho plus support ships are sunk plus ninety planes destroyed for loss of twenty U.S. planes.*

25 August 1942	Germans take Mozdoc in the Caucasus, their closest point to the Russian oilfields.
8 September	RAF bombs Düsseldorf.
10 September	Germans reach outskirts of Stalingrad.
10 September	Germans attack a British Arctic convoy of forty cargo ships plus destroyer escorts en route Russia. Thirteen merchantmen lost plus destroyer HMS Somali *plus heavy minesweeper HMS* Leda. *Germans lose forty planes and four U-boats.*
12 September	British passenger liner Laconia *with 1,500 Italian POWs on way to Canada is sunk by U-boat.*
13 September	British land/sea attack on Tobruk and German supply lines. Destroyers HMS Zulu *and HMS* Sikh *and light cruiser HMS* Coventry *are lost. Over two hundred Royal Marines die.*
22 September	Hitler's army chief of staff, General Halder, is sacked and replaced by General Zeitzler.

Chapter XV Dad's a Soldier *June-September 1942*

Oh, what a shock. Our dad was so surprised when that government letter arrived to say he was being called into the army, and must report for military service!

He was not only shocked, but angry.

"Why me?" he demanded to know.

"There are plenty of young men walking about in civvies."[38]

"I done my share . . ." etc., etc.

"What about Mr. King next door?"

Mr. King next door was a carpenter with a job in a war factory, and not likely to be called up. A "reserved occupation" his work was called.

---

[38] Civilian clothing.

I liked the idea of our dad being a soldier and did not understand why he was protesting. He had four deep scars, each the size of a shilling piece, on his upper arm. The army doctor did that to him in the last war, in case of smallpox. As far as I was concerned, that proved our dad must have been a brave soldier.

*   *   *   *   *

The letter ordered him to report for basic training at an army barracks in Woking, Surrey. But nothing could be taken for granted at the Schofields.

"He might decide not to go!" our mother in her worried voice confided.

*   *   *   *   *

About this time, young Alan Tebbs approached our mother as we three were walking past his house at the top of our road.

"Would George and Eileen like to go to my Sunday school?" he enquired.

We answered yes, we should.

"What a kind idea of Alan's," I thought. Only after we joined did I learn about Wadham Hall Sunday School's offer of prizes for those pupils who recruited the most new members. Never mind, we were glad he introduced us to Sunday school.

*   *   *   *   *

Mother was right. About Dad deciding not to join the army, I mean. He packed a suitcase and went off to stay in the country with his Uncle Bill, until the war was over!

Greatuncle Bill and Aunt Clara kept a big public house at Hornchurch Essex, and to our way of thinking, Hornchurch[39] was deep in the country. In fact it is ten miles east of Walthamstow, as the Spitfire flies. Anyway, Dad went off to the country, and that weekend Mum and we, two children, went to visit him. Greatuncle Bill's pub had a very big saloon bar, a restaurant, and bedrooms upstairs. It was a nice place; we had stayed there before.

The only thing I did not like about Hornchurch was Aunt Clara. It was not because she was bad or unkind in any way. She was just big and noisy. She was a big woman in every dimension, up and around, and her once blond hair was somehow kept piled high on top of her head. The kind of person who could unintentionally frighten a young, or not so young, child. To make matters worse, she was a slobbery kisser! Since she was also a late riser, I did not have to suffer her all day long. Auntie rarely came downstairs before noon.

Staff and family took their meals in the kitchen all seated at one very long, scrubbed white wooden table. Aunt Clara at one end, Uncle Bill at the other. Maids, cooks, barmen, and anyone else, at all stages in between. Why they sat me at her end of the table, I never understood. "Here, Georgie, you can sit next to Auntie Clara," Mum and others would say as they pushed and manoeuvered me into place.

So there I sat, quiet and motionless while Aunt Clara shouted orders, banged the table to emphasise her arguments, and roared with laughter at her own jokes!

Greatuncle Bill was a normal-sized, quiet gentleman who

---

[39] During the Battle of Britain, Hornchurch Royal Air Force station was one of the headquarters of Fighter Command and suffered heavy damage from German attacks.

went about his business of managing his business, seemingly unruffled by his wife's antics!

Auntie Clara was not only a late riser but also a late "go to bedder," who was able to attract a circle of late-night, after-hours drinkers around her.

On our first night at the pub, just such a gathering were sitting in a small room downstairs. I was there too, along with Mum and Dad and some people unknown to me. The main bars were in darkness, and the little group engaged in quiet conversation when Auntie screamed.

"There's a man out in the bar! He's looking at us from behind the door."

Uncle Bill and a barman went to look for the supposed intruder. They switched on lights and looked around before declaring there was no one. Uncle Bill assured her there was no burglar, and she eventually calmed down.

It was a scary moment for me and brought to mind a story my parents had told us about an incident that had happened several years before.

Mum and Dad were riding in a car with Bill and Clara. It was late at night on a dark country road when Auntie ordered her husband to "*Stop the car.*"

"There's a ghost standing in the middle of the road!" she said. Poor Uncle Bill had to get out of the car, stand in the headlight beams, and convince her there was no ghost!

*   *   *   *   *

I was not sorry when it was time to go home again, but sad that Dad did not come with us. He was fast becoming a disappointment.

Luckily, my disillusionment was short-lived. At the end of the week, Dad did come home. He had decided to join the army after all.

I did not see or hear our dad leave the house. It must have been very early in the morning, and he did not say good-bye to me. Well, maybe he did, but I was just too sleepy to remember.

The next few days were difficult at home, with Mum shouting at us for every little thing and always looking out of the front room window. She several times sent me running to the corner of our road to see if the postman was in sight.

She regained her calm somewhat when the long-awaited letter arrived from our dad. The envelope was hurriedly torn open as we, children, looked up at her silently, anxiously awaiting news. And according to Mum, the word was good. Two weeks CB (that meant confined to barracks) for being late to report.

"Not bad. Could have been worse," was her only comment.

We were soon invited to visit Dad at the Woking camp. The army was having an open day for families, so on the appointed day, in our best Sunday clothes, off we went on the train to Woking.

We knew one other new soldier at that camp. A Jewish gentleman, who, until very recently, had been one of our insurance men. It had not been many weeks since our mum got some eggs on the black market for him, and she told us that Jews have to eat eggs and matzos at Passover.

Anyway, Dad had been told about him and it was arranged that we meet on visitor's day at the camp.

*   *   *   *   *

Our dad was a big disappointment in army uniform. His coarse brown khaki tunic, buttoned up to the neck, looked as if it had been made to measure for somebody else. The contrast was all the more noticeable because he was normally such a smart dresser.

Never mind, we were pleased and excited to see him just the same. He took us into the canteen for refreshments, and to sit down. This was a big camp, and a lot of walking was involved in looking around. There must have been hundreds of men on the station, and one of them was black. Right there sitting drinking tea in the canteen was a black soldier. I stared. This was the first real life African[40] I had ever seen close to. On the stage, or at the pictures, yes, but this was a first.

*   *   *   *   *

We met our old insurance man. He was being visited by his wife and son, who was a bit younger than me. We spent the rest of the day with them. It turned out to be a fine day, and we, children, were able to play in the grounds for a while. But the time passed so quickly and all too soon came the hour to catch that train for home.

*   *   *   *   *

Even when our dad was a civilian and at home, he was not at home much . . . if you follow me.

Now he was a soldier and not at home at all, he was sadly missed. Especially by me. The house felt empty without him, and Granny Chapman's failing health did not ease the pall of gloom hanging over everything.

Mother was miserable most of the time. Perhaps she was worried about Granny. She said she was short of money now that Dad was only getting army pay. I did not understand how that could be.

Soon after our dad left for the army, Mum took down a large suitcase that had been on top of their bedroom wardrobe. She opened the case to show me its contents. I

---

[40] I never learned if he was African, or West Indian, but regiments raised in the West Indies, and British Colonies in Africa served with distinction in the Middle East, and fighting the Japs in Burma. Since this man was at Woking, he must have (a) come over on his own ticket and volunteered, or (b) been resident in the UK and conscripted.

could not believe my eyes when I saw what was inside. It was full of money! Bundles and bundles of pound notes!

Mother told me it was Dad's capital to start in business again when the war was over. We could not spend it, and we must never tell anyone. I never did tell, but wondered why she told me at all. Next time passing my parents bedroom, I glanced up at the wardrobe. The suitcase was gone. I never asked where.

*   *   *   *   *

Granny Chapman's attitude to hospitals was hard for me to understand. For me, a hospital was where sick people went to get better. Granny was coming from another place, another generation, what in later years would be called another socio-economic level. For her, hospitals were forbidding places, where diseased, very old, or incurably ill people went to die! They must be avoided at all costs.

When Granny's bad days got worse and more frequent, Mum called the doctor. Our regular family doctor was away in the army, and a stranger, an older man, arrived at the house. He seemed a nice gentleman, and he spoke to Granny privately. What he said was not met with her approval. He advised a hospital stay.

I did not know what, if anything, was decided. Mother paid the doctor, and he left.

*   *   *   *   *

Only once before in my life had I seen the inside of a hospital. A long, long time ago, when I was very little, our dad was taken into a Hackney hospital with a broken nose! When Mum and a family group went to visit him next day, we were stopped at the door to the men's ward.

"No children allowed inside," a nursing sister with a sour face and a stiff white uniform bellowed at me.

I was left standing alone at the entrance to the cold, disinfectant-smelling, white-tiled ward for what felt like a long wait. It was noisy big Aunt Clara who eventually came out. She picked me up, tucked me under her arm, and ran the length of the men's ward, to cheers and whistles from some of the patients. At Dad's bedside, she ordered, "Kiss your father," before running back the length of the ward with me under her arm and nursing sister close behind!

*   *   *   *   *

Schooldays at Chapel End were not much fun. I was in Mr. Calloway's class. He was a very thin, balding, bespectacled gentleman, whose strong voice filled the classroom. He spoke slowly and deliberately, as if carefully choosing every word. He walked slowly up and down the aisles between rows of desks and punished any boy not paying attention by grabbing the back of that boy's head and pushing it down to seat level. There followed a hard slap to the "rump." Mr. Calloway's voice never wavered during this exercise, and his lecture continued as if nothing had happened. Luckily, my stay in this class was a brief one, and I was never punished.

Girls, of course, did not suffer corporal punishment.

To add to the misery of it all, school was cold. A note had been sent to each and every parent, advising them of the fuel shortage. Wear more clothing, we were told. The school cannot keep the boilers fired all the time.

My favorite teacher announced that he was leaving. All out of the blue, at morning assembly and right after prayers, Mr. Ling told us he was being called into the army. All the boys of the junior school were sorry to hear that news.

Mr. Ling did come to visit us a few weeks later. He was a military policeman: a "redcap."

*   *   *   *   *

In her turn, Granny Chapman was being taken away, too. An ambulance with a nurse inside came to the front gate. Not the kind of nurse with a stiff white outfit, but the kind with a dark serge tailored costume and pork pie hat. She went with our mum into Granny's room, and when they all came out, Gran was wearing a hospital dressing gown over a thick nightshirt. They must have taken away her clothes. Then the nurse called the driver, and between them they took Gran to the vehicle outside.

She did not say good-bye to me. She did not say anything, but just stared ahead with a sort of unseeing expression. It was clear that she had been crying.

Mother went to the hospital in the ambulance with Granny.

A few days later Mum, my sister, and I went to visit Granny Chapman in the hospital. Walthamstow hospitals are much nicer than Hackney ones, but even so, they are not the kind of places where one wants to spend much time.

Granny was propped up in bed, staring vacantly ahead at nothing in particular. Mother kept on talking to her, but it did not look as though Granny was listening or understanding much. Our visit had been a miserable one.

On the next visiting day, and the one after that, Mother went alone, refusing to take us children with her.

A letter arrived from the hospital. It said that Gran was seriously ill, and enclosed a card to allow Mother to see her at any hour of the day, not just regulation visiting times.

Within the week came a telegram saying Granny was dead.

It should not have been a surprise, but our mum cried a lot.

Granny Schofield and Dad's youngest sister, Aunt Rose, came to stay for a few days to help Mum with the funeral arrangements.

It came as a disappointment for me not to be allowed to go to the funeral. Our mum asked Aunt Rose to take us three children (including her own little boy, our cousin Alan) out of the house for the afternoon.

As badly as I wanted to go to the funeral, conscience told me not to bother Mum at this time.

We, children, arrived back at our house in time to see the soberly dressed mourners leaving for home. Of Granny Chapman's four sisters and two brothers, only the eldest, Eliza, was still living. She hugged our mum as she left the house.

"You've done your duty as a daughter," she said.

CHAPTER XVI

23 September 1942	*British/Dominian forces enter Tananarive, Madagascar.*
About 25 September	*RAF Mosquitoes attack Gestapo HQ in Oslo.*
10 October	*Six hundred planes of the Luftwaffe based in South Italy start ten-day nonstop assault on Malta.*
11 October	*In night battle off Guadalcanal, the Jap heavy cruiser Furutaka plus three destroyers are sunk. One U.S. destroyer is lost.*
23 October	*General Montgomery, with three armoured (one thousand tanks) plus seven infantry divisions (one hundred and fifty thousand men) plus seven hundred RAF warplanes plus naval support, opens major offensive from el Alamein, against German/Italian armies under General Stumme.*
PM 24 October	*General Stumme dies of heart attack. General Rommel called from his sickbed in Germany to reassume command in Egypt.*
26 October	*In air battle east of Guadalcanal, carrier USS Hornet is sunk.*
27-31 October	*German and Italian tanks make fierce and repeated counterattacks, only to suffer heavy losses, at Libyan frontier.*

End of October 1942	*Off coast of Egypt. An officer and two ratings from destroyer HMS Petard scramble aboard sinking sub U559 and salvage code books and enigma coding machine. The officer Lieutenant Anthony Fasson with A. B. Colin Glazier die in this operation. All three are decorated for bravery.*
3 November	*Rommel's army begins retreat westward. Hitler sends orders forbidding any retreat and demands a fight to the last man.*
5 November	*French govovernor-general of Madagascar surrenders to British.*
7 November	*Rommel's deputy General von Thoma along with nine Italian generals have been captured. Four German and eight Italian divisions cease to exist. Thirty thousand prisoners are taken, plus three hundred and fifty tanks, four hundred guns, plus transports. Churchill later described the Battle of Alamein as the war's turning point, or the "Hinge of Fate."*
7-8 November	*Operation Torch. Allied landings in French North Africa. American troops suffer first casualties in European theatre when they exchange fire with French army.*
10 November	*Churchill, speaking in London about el Alamein: "This is not the end, it is not even the beginning of the end, but it is the end of the beginning."*
11 November	*Eighth Army crosses Libyan frontier.*
11 November	*Hitler orders occupation of Vichy France. From now on all France is under direct German rule.*
13 November	*British enter Tobruk.*
19 November	*Russians attack north and south of Stalingrad in a pincer movement. Hitler refuses permission to retreat.*
22 November	*Off Guadalcanal, cruiser USS Juneau is*

	lost with over six hundred men.
23 November 1942	Two Russian armies meet trapping the German Sixth Army that was itself encircling Stalingrad.
27 November	On orders of Adm. Jean de Laborde, French fleet are scuttled at Toulon harbour. Two battleships, two battlecruisers, six cruisers, thirty destroyers, sixteen submarines are sunk.
30 November	In sea battle off Guadalcanal, cruiser USS Northampton is lost.
4 December	In raid on Naples, RAF bombs and sinks Italian cruiser Muzio Attendolo.
12 December	Germans fail in a desperate attempt to relieve the besieged Sixth Army at Stalingrad.
12 December	British commandos land near Bordeaux, by submarine and canoe, and sink eight ships with limpet mines.
24 December	Admiral Darlan C in C French forces in North Africa is murdered by a student in Algiers.
31 December	RAF bombs Ruhr.

Chapter XVI Life without Father *September-December 1942*

We had two pieces of good news for the end of the year. First, that Dad would be home on leave for Christmas, and second, the club would be having a big party. Dad told us he had made an arrangement with another soldier, a Scotchman, who preferred the New Year to Christmas holidays.

Dad did write to us, of course. And we wrote to him. Inside every envelope, he sent to Mum, there were two small folded notes. One for me and one for my sister, and very often these folded notes held two silver three-penny bits. Our dad was stationed in Kilmarnock. In Scotland, Dad told us, the little silver coins still circulated.

We did, by prearrangement with him, telephone our dad in Scotland. Mother booked the trunk call an hour or so in advance, and at the appointed time we three stood around the telephone. We heard the operators connect the line to each other as the call moved through the exchanges, up the wire to Kilmarnock. It was exciting to hear Dad's scratchy voice, and we, children, shouted into the speaker that we looked forward to seeing him. He told our mum exactly which train he would be catching.

When our dad reached home for that first fourteen days' leave, he must have carried his entire kit with him. He had a heavy pack strapped to his back, and another, with respirator, strapped to his chest. On top of the backpack was a rolled rubber ground sheet, and attached to his heavy belt was a water bottle, a scabbard and bayonet, and a few other unidentifiable objects. A heavy, vintage rifle was slung on his shoulder, and he carried an overcoat, a kit bag, and a steel helmet!

Our dad was now a private in the Royal Army Service Corps (RASC)—that part of the military dealing with transport. He was, in other words, a lorry driver.

He smelled of blanco[41] and looked like a real soldier.

"What did you bring us?" was his children's first question.

One toy he did bring me to play with, although not intentionally, was his rifle. That big old heavy rifle,[42] with a bolt action too hard for me to pull back. It was really too cumbersome for me to carry; but that did not stop me. I lugged that thing upstairs, downstairs, and up the back garden to our Anderson shelter's sandbags. Oh, what a lark.

I did not understand at the time, but these old guns were being given to noncombatants. The "real" infantry got the new stuff.

---

[41] A cleaning material used by soldiers on canvas belts, leggings, etc.

[42] The Lee-Enfield .303 was standard army issue from 1902.

We, children, expected our dad to come into the house and straightaway play games and tell stories with us "little 'uns," but it was not to be. He stood with his back against the kitchen sink and his arms around our mum as they gazed into each other's eyes. Grown-ups can be soppy at times. Then Mother announced that he must be very tired after his long journey and he was going to take a nap, just for a little while. It made sense; he must have been very tired.

We, kids, went out to play in the garden. Mum and Dad took their tea upstairs for him to take a rest.

*   *   *   *   *

Mrs. Vinson, the club manager's wife, was the Christmas party organizer. For days and days before the event, she was excitedly telling us all about the generosity of the club's friends. How people had obtained scarce foodstuffs, "under the counter," to give towards the upcoming party.

It was late on Christmas afternoon that we left home for the club. We were among the first arrivals because our mum was a food contributor. We found Mrs. Vinson beautifully dressed in a full-length evening gown.

Our mum and dad wore ordinary clothes. Mum, a nice frock, and Dad a smart civvy[43] suit.

Our dad always ordered his suits from a very high-class Jewish bespoke tailor in Whitechapel. The shop was not there anymore. It had been destroyed early in the Blitz, but I supposed Dad would soon find its new premises as soon as the war was over.

Mother, too, used to have clothes made by a ladies' tailoress in the City. Not her stays; for that a woman used to come to our house to fit her.

As more people came into the club in ordinary attire,

---

[43]   Civilian.

Mrs. Vinson changed her mind and changed her dress for a short one.

It was such a good party, with lots of good things to eat and drink. We had sweets and cakes, and the men smoked cigarettes from big boxes being passed around. Not the unknown cigarette brands that were being sold in the shops nowadays, but real Players, Capstans, and Gold Flake.

Mr. Vinson, it was said, suffered from a glandular disorder that caused him to be excessively overweight. It was also said that as an infantryman in the last war, he had been badly wounded and still bore the scars.

I think it was he who proposed the toast.

"Everybody got a glass?" he asked.

"Let's remember all our boys who are away from home tonight."

"To our boys," he said with glass raised.

"Our boys," everyone replied.

It was a serious, solemn moment. Then everything went back to normal.

The piano player struck up a tune, and people started dancing. We did laugh to see our dad dancing with a very fat lady that we did not know. Our mum quietly rebuked me and my sister, saying it was not nice to laugh at people.

We would soon have another chance to laugh at others. It was party piece time.

In the recent past, before electric record players, or other "canned" entertainment were common, most people had a party piece. That is a song to sing, or monologue to recite, to entertain the other guests at a party. Of course, if one went to parties with the same people all the time, one heard the same songs and jokes all the time. The club was a good example of this.

The (self-appointed) Master of Ceremonies was announcing the show. First was the stout gentleman in the grey suit and bowler hat. He and his wife always sat quietly together at a separate table and did not mix much with other people. That is why I never knew their name. He always sang "Shine on Harvest Moon," and tonight was no exception.

Then there was Mr. Stark to make us laugh. He would wear a funny old hat, hold a red tablecloth like a matador's cape, and wave an iron poker as a sword, for his version of "The Spaniard Who Blighted My Life." Mr. Stark, a local businessman, was also, what used to be called, a raconteur. He could tell his listeners any story and make it sound entertaining and funny.

One of our most talented performers was a young lady named Rosie who sang to her own piano accompaniment. She always ended her piece with a particular love song. A story, passed around by the clubwomen, said that Rosie had suffered a disappointing love affair, and this had been "their" song. So, as Rosie sang and played her heart out, the women, with sad all-knowing expressions on their faces, nodded sympathetically.

"And now," the MC went on, "a song from Mr. Dick Edge."

Mr. Edge, as always, was smartly dressed in a three-piece tailored suit, but tonight as he stood in the centre of the floor, he removed the jacket. A man's black hat on his head appeared to be a bit too small for him.

He started to sing an Irish song about the boys of O'Flanagan's band.[44] The verse ended with "here's a tribute to Old Ireland and . . . the boys of O'Flanagan's band." The chorus named the instruments and players. "And the drum went bang . . . and the cymbals . . . the old trombone . . . ," As he sang about each instrument he acted out its playing, miming the bass drummer, the cymbalist, the trombonist, et al. He then threw his hat onto the floor and danced a jig around it. His highly polished small black leather shoes just missing the hat with every landing. Mr. Edge was not exactly

---

[44]   In the mid- or late-1940s, Bing Crosby recorded a song entitled "MacNamara's Band." Similar tune. Different words.

tall, nor was he really fat; he was just a big fellow, whose size added to the comic effect of the performance.

There were several verses.

"The Prince of Wales to Ireland came . . ." At the end of the last chorus he did his jig, but this time furiously jumping hard on the hat instead of missing it!

Our mum nudged Dad and asked, "Where's your hat?"

Dad leaned forward to show he was holding his best homburg behind his back.

"I've seen him before," he said.

Did I mention the gentleman who looked a bit like Hitler? He would comb his black hair straight forward in a half fringe and hold a part of his black comb under his nose. With a clicking of heels and a mock Nazi salute, this was his impersonation of old Adolph. Everyone laughed, jeered, boohed, and made rude noises!

There was only one casualty at the party. A man our mum referred to as "Monkey-doodle." It was true that this man walked, sort of bent forward, and his arms looked too long for his sleeves. But, having already told us off for laughing at somebody, why do it herself?

Anyway, Mr. Monkey-doodle fell hard and struck his head on the folded ping-pong table. Some of the men took him to get medical attention at the nearby first-aid post. He was back at the party within the hour, wearing a clean wide white bandage around his head and looking around demanding to know what happened to the beer he'd left behind.

His injury could not have been serious, and as I said, "It was such a good party."

*   *   *   *   *

Fourteen days was a long time at the beginning, but towards the end of Dad's leave it was no time at all! Those last days just raced by.

Before leaving, Dad gave me his instructions. Putting his hand on my shoulder, he said, "You must be the man of the house while I am away, and look after your mother."

I took his order very seriously, swallowed hard, and determined to do just that.

Dad also explained that with the war and everything, it might not be possible to pay for my higher education, as had always been understood. I would just have to pass the examination for a scholarship. Our dad won a scholarship when he was my age. He was Maidstone Street School's top boy for that year and won a place at a trade or craft school, or something. It was all for nothing anyway, since his parents could not afford to let him go. They needed his wages, so at age twelve, instead of high school, he was sent to work in a brewery.

*　　*　　*　　*　　*

As soon as Dad left for Scotland, everything went back to dull and miserable. It was now January, the middle of winter. A time for long dark nights, cold damp weather, pea souper fogs . . . And a return to school.

The clock on the dining room mantelpiece stopped. When Dad was at home, he religiously wound that clock every night, carefully counting the turns of the key to maintain constant spring tension. As soon as Dad left the house, Mum lost interest in the thing and just let it run down.

So many reminders of our dad's presence still haunted the house, the razor strop and shaving mug in the bathroom, for example. He did not take them back with him, saying his new safety razor was easier than the old fashioned stuff to use at the barracks.

He never did go back to his old cutthroat.

*　　*　　*　　*　　*

Nineteen forty-two had been a quiet year for air raids. That would soon change, and it was in this month, our house suffered its first war damage. An antiaircraft shell burst on the kerbstone just opposite our front windows. The explosion made a deafening noise, shattered a lot of glass, and left a big dent in the solid stone kerb.[45] We lost only one window.

"It's the fault of them bloody 'ome Guards on the guns," our mum kept saying, although I doubted that the Home Guard were involved. Council[46] workmen quickly came around and replaced all broken windows with frosted glass.

The year 1943 had opened badly and was to get worse as it went along. Mother announced that since money was short, she had decided to go back to work. It was Mr. Polikoff himself who said she could always return. That was twelve or thirteen years earlier, when Mum left her job to get married.

On the plus side, her going out to work meant that I could now stay to school dinners.

*   *   *   *   *

In second term of the third and final year at Chapel End Junior School, some pupils and classes were reshuffled. I was placed in young Mr. Grainger's class. He was referred to as "young" Mr. Grainger, because his father was also a master at Chapel End. Each age group of children was divided into three classes: "A" was the top class; "B," the middle; and "C," the lowest.

Young Mr. Grainger was master in the C class. He was a thin, pale young man of delicate appearance. In his soft voice, he would patiently and unhurriedly explain his lessons until the slowest learner could understand.

---

[45] A weapon, introduced about this time, was a rocket propelled proximity exploding antiaircraft shell. Its existence was a close secret.

[46] "Council workers" employed by the Walthamstow Borough Council.

Some class teachers allowed their pupils to sit where they liked. Others insisted on a boy-girl arrangement, or some alphabetical order, or "baddies" at the front and "gooders" at the back. Mr. Grainger seated his class in order of academic merit. The best and brightest were seated high at the back of the room, and to the teacher's right. There were five or six rows of twin desks, seating about forty children. The standard of intelligence decreased down the lines of desks until reaching the worst dullards at front and left.

As the newest boy in the class, I was given the second to last desk, front and left.

The boy I was to sit beside, Lenny Fogarty, was the acknowledged school idiot. All the other boys made fun of him. His poor schoolwork was no surprise, as he spent so much time scratching his behind or picking his nose. My new classmate smiled and greeted me as I went to take my place.

"Hello, Schofield," he said, offering his hand to shake. My thoughts ran to where that hand might have been.

"Hello, Fogarty," I answered, enthusiastically patting his shoulder.

There was only one desk in front of mine. It was all that stood between me and complete disgrace.

That desk was occupied by two girls named "Gert" and "Lou." Their full names were probably Gertrude and Louise, but nobody ever addressed them as such. Gert had a harelip and a speech problem; I did not understand everything she said. Lou had a hair problem; the health authorities, at intervals, took her away and shaved her head!

*　　*　　*　　*　　*

Our mum was serious about getting a job. The direction of labour laws now applied to women. No able-bodied adult was allowed to be idle, without a good reason. If you could not find a job, the Department of Labour would find one for you! These strict laws did not apply to women with school-aged children at home, so Mum was not obliged to go.

Mum's visit to her former employer was something of a letdown. Old Mr. Polikoff was no longer there, and the new management did not remember her. The only jobs available were at the bench, at the bottom rate of pay. Mother came home disappointed but not despondent. Within the week, she started war work at a metal factory not far from home. It was hard work, she told us, and we, children, must help with housework and getting the tea ready. We, children, were ready and willing, even if not completely able.

*   *   *   *   *

CHAPTER XVII

January 1943	*"Le Melice," a twenty-five-thousand-strong French police force, is formed to help the Gestapo combat French resistance.*
3 January	*Cruiser Ulpio Traiano is sunk in Palermo harbour by British two-man submarine.*
4 January	*Russians retake Mozdok.*
8 January	*General Rokossovsky offers General von Paulus a "final" chance to surrender his German army trapped at Stalingrad.*
14 January	*Churchill and FDR meet at Casablanca.*
15 January	*General von Löhr's army of Germans, Italians, and Croats start major offensive against Tito's forces in Yugoslavia.*
22 January	*Jap forces are defeated by an Australian/U.S. Army advancing in New Guinea. Seven thousand Japs die.*
31 January	*General von Paulus is promoted to field marshall by Hitler.*
1 February	*Von Paulus defies Hitler's orders and surrenders to Russians. Of 284,000 Germans trapped at Stalingrad, 160,000 are dead. Over thirty thousand evacuated by air. Of ninety thousand prisoners, only about six thousand would survive to return home. (Recent studies put Soviet army casualties at Stalingrad as one million dead.)*

12 February 1943	*British forces enter Tunisia from Libya.*
14 February	*Germans attack U.S. Army at Kasserine Pass and force their retreat back into Algeria. The officer in charge of Tenth Panzers (Count von Stauffenberg) is badly wounded in Tunisia, losing part of his right arm.*
14 February	*Russians retake Rostov.*
14 February	*Operation Loincloth. Three thousand Chindits (British and Ghurka) under Brigade General Wingate infiltrate five hundred miles into Burma from India. Carry out anti-Japanese ambushes and sabotage.*
3 March	*One hundred and seventy-three die at London's Bethnal Green tube station disaster.*
4 March	*Japs, trying to reinforce New Guinea across Bismarck Sea, lose eight merchantmen, four destroyers, one hundred and four planes to U.S./ Australian warplanes.*
4 March	*Four hundred and forty-two RAF bombers hit Essen and the Ruhr.*
5 March	*Reich Commissar of Ukraine Erich Koch speaking at Kiev: "We are a master race, and must remember the lowliest German worker is racially and biologically a thousand times more valuable than the population here."*
6 March	*Rommel retreats with his German/ Italian forces, and suffers heavy losses, after attacks on Eighth Army near Mareth Line, Tunisia.*
6 March	*RAF bombs Essen.*
10 March	*RAF bombs Munich.*
10 March	*German offensive to take city of Kharkov.*
13 March	*Assassination attempt against Hitler by German staff officers at Smolensk but time bomb fails to explode.*

| 18 March 1943 | USAAF bomb submarine pens at Bremen from their base in England. |
| 29 March | After a week of heavy fighting Montgomery's Eighth Army breaks through Mareth Line and inflicts major defeat on German/Italian defenders. |

Chapter XVII The Dreaded Black Book, or Business as Usual *January-April 1943*

> *Hitler has given up playing snooker . . . He can't get the reds down.*
>
> —Gillie Potter, BBC Radio Comedian

Every forenoon, tables and chairs were set up in the school assembly hall, ahead of the hungry mass of children who would burst in at the stroke of twelve. One of these tables, that seated ten, was always commandeered by Robby Maitland's gang. Since I was new to the dining hall, they allowed me to sit with them. Robby's mates were mostly a scruffy lot, but so was I. In the months since Dad joined the army, my ill-fitting school clothes looked the worse for wear. As contemporary slang would have it, I was short on good clobber.[47]

Clothes rationing was easier for grown-ups because good suits and frocks can last a long time. Years and years, if looked after, but growing children outgrow their clothes. Our dress code may have been informal, but our dining mode was rigid and enforced. The days when Mr. Hall had charge of the dining hall were the worst. As he walked between rows of tables, he barked orders like, "Straighten your back, young man," and, "You, sit up straight," and, "No, no, not like that. Hold your knife and fork like this!"

He made one major concession to rationing and the food shortage.

---

[47]   Clothing.

"If there is a food you do not like, you may pass it to the plate of someone who does," Mr. Hall announced. Otherwise, any uneaten food on a plate had better have a good story to go with it.

Things were easier on days when other teachers were in charge.

*　　*　　*　　*　　*

It was during one midday break, I remembered that something needed for the next lesson had been left behind in my desk. Two other boys from my class, plus the Snoad brothers, had the same problem. We all walked back to the classroom only to find the door locked. Mr. Grainger's class was in a separate little building away from the main block, and on ground level. We decided to try a window, and one of us climbed through, lifted the door latch, and let in the other boys.

Of course, young Mr. Grainger found out about it later that afternoon, and we, five culprits, were made to stand up while he gave us a "telling off." If it had been left to Mr. Grainger, it would have ended with a telling off, but Mr. Hall entered the room at that moment.

"What is this?" he demanded to know, and Mr. Grainger dutifully explained.

"I shall deal with this," said Mr. Hall, and we five were marched off to the headmaster's study. There we stood silently to attention as the headmaster delivered his lecture. I stood at one end of the line, and the Snoad boys at the other.

"We do not tolerate indiscipline . . . ," and so on and so on he ranted, all the time waving a cane. The cane, I noticed was not the one he always used as a pointer, but the long, thin punishment cane.

There was still one thing missing from this ritual. The dreaded black punishment book, in which the names of caned boys must be written. It was an indispensable part of the ceremony. Mr. Hall stopped speaking and stood quietly for a moment. Then he reached for the "Black Book"!

The Snoad brothers straight away started to cry. "Oh no, sir, please, sir, oh please, sir," they bawled.

Mr. Hall waved his cane, "Out, out," he ordered the two boys.

They did not need telling twice, but ran, as if for their lives, still crying, as they scurried through the study door.

We, three remaining boys, were told to hold out one hand. We received one sharp stroke of the cane across upturned palms. I felt a bit sick, but did not cry. I refused to let the likes of Mr. Hall make me cry.

I did think the headmaster handled the situation badly. Three boys had been punished for not being cowards. Two boys had been taught the lesson that cowardice does pay.

At home that night I blurted out my tale of woe and injustice to Mother. Mrs. Maitland was often at the school to complain whenever Robby was in trouble. I fully expected Mum to do the same, but instead had to suffer more disappointment.

"If you'd behave your bloody self, you wouldn't get into trouble," was her only comment.

*   *   *   *   *

There seemed to be more air raid alarms lately, and we moved the beds from upstairs to the front room downstairs. Mother thought it safer, because of the raids, to sleep downstairs. The old kitchen table we set in the middle of the room as a place to dive under in an emergency. The easy chairs and the piano went to join the radiogram in the dining room. The aspidistras had long since disappeared.

This arrangement was not only safer but more comfortable. With the fuel shortage, we heated only the kitchen and front room downstairs.

Mother's job at the metal works did not last more than a few weeks; it was listed as "war work," and as she explained to us, "If they put you onto 'permanent staff,' there's no way to leave. Not even if you want to!"[48]

Mother valued her freedom and got a new job with the post office telephone division, in the City of London.

There was one bright spot on my calendar of activities: Wadham Hall Sunday School Bible class on Sunday afternoons with prayers and gospel singing. Hobbies class, followed by prayers and gospel singing, one evening a week. The hobbies taught and practiced were stamp collecting and fretwork for boys, and embroidery and picture making for girls. I, of course, was active in the philately department. I also took my bus and tram ticket collection to show off. My collection of bookmakers and "tote"[49] tickets was less well received.

Wadham Hall was a single-story, rustic-looking wooden building that stood on its own plot of land facing the arterial road. Chapel End School was a stone's throw away.

At the three o'clock Sunday service for children, we all sat in the main hall, but were divided into classes by age and gender. Each class formed by a circle of little chairs, with teachers (sitting on bigger chairs), forming part of the ring.

Boy's classes on one side of the room, girls on the other.

I was, at first, placed in Mr. Smelling's class, along with the other ten-year-old boys. This dark-haired, slightly built, very young man was awaiting his calling up papers from the navy. His parents were also teachers and members of this Plymouth Brethren group.

We did not use hymn books. Well, hardly, because here we did not sing many hymns. At Wadham Hall, we enjoyed rousing choruses, which we sang from chorus books. Here we leaned more to the tambourine style works of Fanny Crosby than the grand organ music of Georg Handel.

---

[48] War work for women aged eighteen to fifty compulsory from May 1943.

[49] Totalizator. Betting tickets issued at race tracks.

*   *   *   *   *

With the warmer weather soon expected, it was time for me to realize a long-held ambition and go into the farming business. Well, not real farming, but keeping chickens. I had done the arithmetic and calculated the cost of chicken feed and the sale price of eggs. Mum agreed that I could spend my own money in this enterprise, and I agreed to do all the work myself.

The next Sunday morning saw me in Petticoat Lane market among the live poultry dealers. The area around the "Lane" had been flattened by heavy bombing during the blitz. Hardly a building was left standing, and all that wide-open space was fine for the market. This was serious business for me, so I had come alone with my cash in my pocket, and my hand in my pocket as protection against thieves.

The moment I saw her sitting alone on what was left of a brick wall, I knew she was the one for me. She was trying to sleep with her head and neck half buried in her deep white feathers. I sidled up to the youth who was leaning against the same half wall, and in a similar state of sloth.

"Whatchaaskin'?" I enquired, nodding towards the sleeping bird and trying to look disinterested.

The fellow sprang to life, no doubt sensing a sale. "Twelve and six,"[50] he answered, "nice pullet."[51]

I decided not to 'bate[52] and just gave him the money. He put the bird into a paper bag with just its head sticking out, and with that I rode straight home on the trolley bus.

"You bloody fool, you paid too much for it," were our mum's first words, "go and ask Mr. Capes if he will come and have a look at it. It looks to me as if it's dying."

---

[50] 12 shillings and 6 pence = £0.625.

[51] Young hen.

[52] Abate; to reduce the price by arguing.

Mr. Capes was a friend of our parents who lived in our road and kept a lot of chickens. We stood my chicken on the outside coal shed for Mr. Capes' inspection.

He did not appear overenthusiastic!

"Have you given it a drink of water?" he asked.

"Oh yes," I assured him as my chicken stood there looking bedraggled, listless, and ready at any moment to fulfill Mum's prophesy and drop dead!

"It was a long journey on the bus. Perhaps it's travel sick." I said in a forlorn attempt to inject some optimism into the proceeding.

Well, the Anderson shelter at the bottom of our garden had been dried out and swept clean by me earlier. A wooden pole was balanced inside to serve as a perch for our new family member. It was fed chicken meal and boiled potato peelings on its own little plate, and I had prepared a box with dry hay inside, ready for the expected eggs. Now all we had to do was wait.

That chicken never had a name; it was just called chicken, but in no time at all, a family member is what it became.[53]

*　　*　　*　　*　　*

It was about this time that I learned of the death of Granny Chapman's friend, old Mrs. Mac. We had not seen or received word from her for some time, but because of the heavy bombing in her part of London, that was to be expected. Many people had been evacuated or forced by circumstances to move away.

It seems old Mrs. Mac (a woman who was afraid of thunderstorms) went into the public air raid shelter . . . and stayed there. The other people, who used the shelter, could not persuade her to leave for any reason! The authorities

---

[53] When shown this manuscript., my sister insisted the chicken did have a name, "Swanny." Well, nobody told me!

were called, and Mrs. Mac was forcibly taken to the hospital, where she died.

It was sad news for me. Poor old Mrs. Mac never hurt anyone; it wasn't fair she should go like that. It wasn't fair.

Chapter XVIII

3-5 April 1943	*Ruhr is heavily bombed by RAF.*
5 April	*USAAF bomb Renault factory near Paris. Two hundred plus French civilians are killed.*
5 April	*USAAF bombers attempting to destroy an aircraft plant near Antwerp hit residential area by mistake. Nearly one thousand Belgian civilians die including two hundred schoolchildren.*
7 April	*Heavy Jap air attacks on Guadalcanal. Destroyer USS Aaron Ward, escort HMNZS Moa, and three cargo ships are lost.*
18 April	*Admiral Yamamoto C in C Jap fleet, and leader of attack on Pearl Harbour, is killed when his plane is ambushed by U.S. fighters over Solomon Islands.*
4 May	*British bound convoy is attacked in Atlantic by thirty strong U-boat pack. Fifteen merchant ships and six U-boats are sunk.*
7 May	*U.S. forces take north Tunisian port of Bizerta.*
7 May	*After fierce resistance by its German/ Italian defenders, Tunis falls to British First Army.*
13 May	*Dispatch from General Alexander to Churchill:*
	"Sir, it is my duty to report that the

	Tunisian campaign is over. All enemy resistance has ceased. We are masters of the North African shores."
14 May 1943	*"Operation Pointblank" approved. British/American bomber offensive from British bases for "destruction and dislocation of the German military and economic system and the undermining of the morale of the German people."*
16 May	*"Dam Busters" led by Wing Cdr. Guy Gibson, eighteen RAF heavy bombers armed with specially designed (by Dr. Barnes Wallis) bouncing bombs, breach two of three dams serving the Ruhr. Eight bombers are shot down. Fifty-six of the 153 crewmen die. In the floods caused by the bombing, over 1,200 die.*
17 May	*The first convoy since 1941, to cross the Mediterranean, leaves Gibraltar and arrives at Alexandria 26 May without loss.*
24 May	*Heavy raids by RAF on Dortmund and the Ruhr.*
26 May	*Meeting in Washington, FDR and WSC agree that "the Anglo-American exchange of information on the atomic bomb, suspended for more than a year because of mutual suspicions, should be resumed, and that henceforth the enterprise should be considered a joint one to which both countries would contribute their best endeavours."*[54]
29 May	*Following an RAF raid on Wuppertal in the west German industrial belt, town suffers firestorm killing 2,500 people.*
30 May	*U.S. forces in taking island of Attu (Bering Sea) find 2,500 dead Japanese. The last survivors having committed mass suicide. Six hundred Americans die in this action.*
June	*U.S. Marines under General MacArthur*

54   Sir Martin Gilbert, *The Second World War*, chap. 22, p. 434.

	make steady gains moving island to island in the Solomans.
1 June 1943	*Film star Leslie Howard is killed when plane taking him to London from Lisbon is shot down.*
1 June	*Luftwaffe opens attacks against Kursk.*
11 June	*British forces capture Italian island of Pantelleria and other islands in the Sicilian Channel. Eleven thousand Italian prisoners are taken.*
July	*Air offensive against Sicily opens with four thousand Allied warplanes.*
5 July	*Death of Gen. Wladyslaw Sikorski C in C Free Polish forces. Head of government in exile. Plane crash off Gibraltar.*
5 July	*"Operation Citadel." Germans open major offensive against Kursk salient. The nearly 200-mile front is site of the biggest land battle in all history, as German and Russian forces fight with 6,000 tanks, 4,000 warplanes, and 2,200,000 soldiers (1,300,000 Soviet; 900,000 German). The Soviet command anticipated and prepared for the German advance, counterattack on 12 July. Orel at northern end of the front falls to Russians on 5 August. Kharkov, two hundred miles south, is captured on the twenty-third. From now until end of the war, German forces are in retreat. (A small number of French pilots are engaged on "both" sides in this battle!)*
10 July	*Allied forces invade Sicily.*
PM 10 July	*Syracuse, first Axis city to fall to Allies is taken by British forces.*
24 July	*Mussolini is dismissed ending twenty-one years as Italian dictator.*
24 July	*Operation Gomorrah opens as 790 RAF bombers unload 2,300 tons of bombs on Hamburg. Using new direction finding equipment (H2S), and new radar*

	jamming device (window), only twelve bombers are lost. Four such attacks carried out until 3 August and over forty thousand civilians die.
25 July 1943	Mussolini arrested. Replaced by Marshal Pietro Badoglio.
1 August	U.S. flying fortresses cross Mediterranean Sea to bomb oil refineries at Ploesti Rumania, of the 175 planes, 54 are lost with 532 crewmen.
5 August	British reach Catania, Sicily.
11 August	Germans start evacuation from Sicily.
17 August	U.S. forces enter Messina, the last Axis held town in Sicily.
Day 17 August	Five hundred USAAF bombers hit engineering works at Schweinfurt and Regensburg deep inside Germany. Sixty planes are lost.
Night 17 August	Heavy RAF raid on rocket establishment at Peenemünde. Of seven hundred plus killed on the ground, most are foreign forced labourers.
23 August	Seven hundred RAF heavy bombers raid Berlin area.
27 August	Tito holds his first Yugoslav National Assembly at Jajce, Bosnia.
28 August	Death of King Boris III of Bulgaria under mysterious circumstances and following a row with Hitler.
30 August	Six hundred RAF heavy bombers raid Berlin area.
30 August	Internal German government report list their own casualties on Russian front. To date: 550,000 killed, 2,000,000 wounded.
3 September	British troops of Montgomery's Eighth Army land in Italy.
PM 3 September	Italian government signs armistice with Allies. To go into effect in five days.
5 September	A U.S./Australian parachute brigade capture Nazdab, New Guinea.
8 September	On the announcement of Italian

	capitulation, Hitler orders German occupation of Italy.
Night 8 September 1943	*As per Allied directions, the bulk of the Italian fleet leave Genoa and La Spezia for Malta. In daylight off Sardinia, battleship* Roma *is hit by German-guided bomb and sinks with 1,500 men including C in C Admiral Bergamini. Battleship* Italia *is damaged. Remainder of fleet are met by British warships AM tenth and escorted to Malta.*
9 September	*Germans occupy Athens after disarming the Italian garrison.*
9 September	*British paratroopers capture Taranto naval base.*
9 September	*U.S. troops take Salerno.*
10 September	*In Memo Churchill to Admiral Cunningham reference surrender of Italian fleet: "They shall be received in kindly and generous manner. I feel sure this will be in accordance with your sentiments."*
10 September	*Germans take Rome.*
12 September	*Germans abandon Isle of Capri.*
12 September	*Ninety German commandos land by gliders, capture mountaintop prison to free Mussolini, and take him (eventually) to Hitler's HQ at Rastenburg.*
17 September	*Brig. Fitzroy Maclean parachutes into Yugoslavia. Takes charge British mission to Tito.*
20 September	*Battleship* Tirpitz, *at anchor in a Norwegian fjord, is badly damaged by British midget submarines.*
24 September	*Germans abandon Smolensk.*
Early October	*Australian forces in New Guinea take Finschhafen as Japs suffer heavy casualties.*
13 October	*Government of Italy declares war on Germany.*

14 October 1943	Two hundred twenty-eight USAAF flying forts attack ball-bearing factory at Schweinfurt. Sixty-two bombers are lost with one-hundred-plus aircrew.
23 October	In naval action off Channel Islands, cruiser HMS Charybdis is torpedoed and sunk. Over five hundred men die.
November	Sir Oswald and Lady Moseley are released from detention on health grounds.
November	USAAF now have fighter protection for daylight raids over Germany.
6 November	Russian forces capture Kiev.
15 November	After heavy fighting, Germans retake Aegean island of Leros from British/Italian forces.
16 November	USAAF bombers based in Britain bomb hydroelectric station and heavy water plant in Norway.
20 November	At Tarawa Atoll, Gilbert Islands. After a three-day assault by U.S. forces all five thousand fanatic Jap defenders are dead. One thousand of the five thousand landing forces die in this action. Carrier USS Lisome Bay is torpedoed and sunk with over six hundred of its nine hundred men.
22-26 November	Cairo Conference. FDR WSC Chiang Kaishek.
25 November	Australian forces capture Sattelburg mountain area of New Guinea after weeklong battle.
28 November	Tehran Conference. FDR WSC Stalin.
1 December	The Soviet leader agrees to enter the war against Japan: "The moment Germany is defeated."
15 December	U.S. forces land on New Britain in Bismarck Arch.
16 to end of December	RAF makes repeated raids on Berlin inflicting and suffering heavy casualties.
25 December	This evening battleship Scharnhorst plus

	five destroyers under R. Adm Bey, sail from Alten Fjord Norway, to attack a British convoy to Russia. (It was the last time a German fleet ever put to sea.)
27 December 1943	In action with British convoy escorts and later with battleship HMS Duke of York under Admiral Fraser, Scharnhorst is sunk. Of German ships' complement of 1,970, only thirty-six survive.
28 December	Canadian and British troops take Ortona on Italian Adriatic coast.

Chapter XVIII Holidays at Home, or Run for Cover *March-December 1943*

One good thing about this spring, it would be my last term in the junior school. Whether I passed the scholarship examination and went up to a higher school, or failed and went upstairs to the senior school, this was my last term with Mr. Hall. I had already taken the examinations. It was just a matter of waiting for the postwoman[55] with the result. Those candidates who passed were notified by mail, and the failures just ignored.

Another good thing about this spring is that it would soon be time for Dad's summer leave. Mum planned to leave her post office job just before Dad's arrival, so we should all be on holiday together. She explained to us that the journey morning and night was too long, and what with the air raids and everything, she would look for another job nearer home, after Dad went back.

* * * * *

It was during these evenings that I became an avid wireless listener. Our radiogram was in the cold, no longer

[55] Most postal routes were now "manned" by women.

used, dining room along with other damp furniture, and fast going out of tune piano. That did not deter me from sitting curled up on the cold floor, with one ear pressed against the radio speaker, and spending hours being educated, informed, and entertained.

The radiogram, that big piece of furniture with its polished walnut veneer finish and "lift up" lid, had been a centre of pride only a few years before. Neighbours were invited in to see and admire the electric, seventy-eight RPM turntable that could switch itself off at the end of each record. And the wireless part, with all those foreign stations, marked on different wave lengths. It stood on the floor, opposite the door, and beside the glass case displaying Mother's best china. It was the first thing one saw when entering the dining room.

"And you don't have to wind it up," we, children, were quick to tell visitors.

Only one fellow was unimpressed. Our cousin Reggie, who, after a long thoughtful inspection, pronounced, "You can't get television on it then?"

* * * * *

What radio shows induced me to suffer such discomfort? There were several favourites, including *The Brains Trust*. An odd choice for an eleven-year-old perhaps, but I paid careful attention as the panel answered questions on all sorts of subjects mailed in by listeners.

On the panel of experts sat Dr. Joad, Professor Huxley, Commander Campbell, and a transient who was usually an expert in something or another. Whatever the question, each speaker had a particular way of dealing with it. For example, Dr. Joad, the philosopher, who had a distinctive, high-pitched voice, would say, "Well, of course, it all depends on what you mean by . . ." There followed a discourse on the pros and cons of the matter. He seldom answered the question.

Commander Campbell RN (ret) was an old sailor. His answers might begin, "I remember once when I was in . . ." Followed by an entertaining story, about his travels and adventures.

Professor Huxley, the scientist, would answer concisely and logically—if the question indeed had an answer. Most of these subjects were, of course, beyond my intellect, but I managed to convince myself that I understood.

There is only one of these questions that I still remember; the rest have long been forgotten. A listener wrote to ask, "Are we better men than our fathers?"

I listened attentively to the debate that followed. Today, a panel of experts would not be required because I know the answer to that question. It is *no*.

*   *   *   *   *

I also enjoyed the light music concerts, and the comedy shows, the symphony concerts being still away in my future. *Happidrome* was a Sunday night show, popular with a lot of youngsters. It was set in an imaginary variety theatre where real acts were introduced by a trio of North Country comics playing the parts of manager, stage manager, and pageboy. Mondays would hear my schoolmates telling and retelling the jokes, and imitating "Enoch," the page. I think my enthusiasm for this show was enhanced by the fact that I had seen and knew from real life visits to the Empire and Palace theatres, many of the music hall acts introduced.

The Happidrome was the very antithesis of *The Brains Trust*!

Almost all radio broadcasts came from the BBC. No commercial stations existed in England, and the old Radio Luxemburg was in German hands.

There were the American Forces and the Canadian Forces Network, but they broadcast only at special times, and we did not listen regularly.

No, it was the BBC Home Service, or BBC Light Programme, or nothing! The television service was suspended for the duration of war.

*   *   *   *   *

My favourite aunt, Lylie, had bad news in March, when two of her relatives died in the Bethnal Green tube station disaster. They were among the more than a hundred and seventy people killed in a panic rush for the steep steps of the underground shelter entrance. Many of the victims were mothers and children.

There had been no bomb, no explosion; it was a false alarm, and they all died, suffocated in the crush.

Our mum tried to remind me who the couple were, and said that I did know them. But I could not remember them at all. My sadness was for dear Aunt Lylie.

*   *   *   *   *

It was our mum's suggestion that we buy a second chicken so as to be company for the first one. A funny thing about Mum was her fear of animals. She could handle dogs and cats well enough, but had trouble getting close to any other creature, including chickens. She said that she liked our chicken, but just could not get too near or "pick her up."

I was sent down the "Lane" to buy another bird and returned with a young Rhode Island Red of undetermined gender. The two chickens seemed to get along, and they both became family pets! My sister liked them too, and she spent time feeding and playing with the pair.

That was a great moment when I found the first egg in chicken's hay box. It was a very small egg, and I cupped it in both hands and cautiously, carefully took it to show Mother. She continued to lay eggs, did our chicken, not every day but two or three times a week, this was at a time when the egg ration was two per week per person. That was the summer ration allowance, in winter it was half that.

*   *   *   *   *

As the end of the term drew nearer, it became clear that I had not passed the scholarship examination. Other candidates had been notified. I had not.

Our mum was not only disappointed, but angry.

"You bloody fool," she kept saying.

"Now what am I going to tell your father?"

I kept out of her way as much as possible, and that was not easy!

*   *   *   *   *

Our dad's fourteen-day leave came and went very quickly. We did pack a lot into it, but as always, there was not enough time for everything Dad wanted or had planned to do. We saw some shows, went dog racing, visited the West End, visited the club, visited lots of relatives. He, at no time, mentioned my failures at school.

A film showing at that time in London was a sound version of Charlie Chaplin in *The Gold Rush*. Our dad was particularly keen to see this one. He remembered seeing it years before as a silent picture. We all went to a West End cinema for this film, and it did make us laugh. And I learned where Dad got the comic ideas for his "eating a gramophone record" trick when Charlie ate the boot.

*   *   *   *   *

"Before the war" was a much used phrase in those days. It was the opening line of so many conversations. "Before the war" seemed such a long time ago, when we spent summer holidays by the sea. When we packed our bathing costumes, buckets, and spades, and our dad would take us to Bogner Regis for one week each year. He could only manage a short break because summer was the flat racing season, and his busiest time for business.

Now, Mum and Dad laughed as they talked about the boarding house in Bognor and the guest who complained about breakfast. The young man in question did not like the monotony of eggs and bacon every morning.

"Where is he now?" Mum chuckled.

"I'll bet he'd be only too pleased to get eggs and bacon today!"

For our second seaside holiday of each summer, Mum and Granny Chapman and we, two children, used to enjoy the pleasures of Clacton-on-Sea. We always stayed at the same boarding house, and Dad would come to visit with us on Sundays.

A wartime government billboard slogan urged everyone to "Holiday at Home," and that is what we did. As I said, "before the war" was a long time ago. Now most beaches were closed to the public, covered with barbed wire, tank traps, pillboxes, and even mines! There was no chance of a seaside holiday this year. We went rowing on the lake at Epping Forest instead.

We all went to the railway station with Dad to see him off. Before leaving the house, he again put a hand on my shoulder and started to tell me how I must be the man of the house, etc., etc.

"How can I?" I interrupted.

"THEY WON'T DO AS THEY'RE TOLD!"

Dad no longer traveled with his entire kit when he came home on leave. With just a kit bag and a small attaché case, the four of us went by bus to Euston station. One of Dad's brothers-in-law, Uncle Sid, who now worked at this station, offered to meet us to get a seat for Dad. That six-hour journey was hard enough with a seat. Standing or even sitting on a kit bag in the cold train corridor would have been uncomfortable indeed. With wartime restrictions, there were no restaurant or bar carriages either.

We arrived early on the right platform at the right spot, but the crowd of uniformed men grew and grew, with soldiers, sailors, and airmen everywhere we looked, plus a few civilians, WAAFs, WRNS, and ATS[56] girls. A mass of people all waiting for the same train to arrive at the terminal.

Uncle Sid was a thin, wiry older man and this was his wartime job. It was a surprise when he arrived, as I had never seen him in LMS[57] uniform before. He took Dad's small brown attaché case and told him to follow as best he could.

As the heavy steam engine held its breath to shunt the long train, it slowed to walking pace before stopping at the buffers. The train was still moving quickly as Uncle Sid elbowed his way through the crowd that was itself moving forward towards the platform's edge. With a "Mind your backs please," he was soon standing on the running board, opening a carriage door, and disappearing inside to "reserve" a corner seat.

In a way, it was a good thing there were so many strange people about. It was embarrassing to see Mum and Dad kiss good-bye, especially if she started to cry. I was glad none of my friends were there to see it.

*   *   *   *   *

There was a vacant block of land in front of Euston station, a bombsite perhaps, that had been enclosed by a heavy, high wooden fence. A few uniformed policemen were pacing its perimeter.

I found a crack in a plank, or a knothole, or something, and peered through. Inside the enclosure scruffy men, all

---

[56] Women's Auxiliary Air Force, Women's Royal Naval Service, and Auxiliary Training Service (later Women's Royal Army Corps).
[57] London Midland and Scottish Railway Co.

dressed alike, stood around, or sat on the rough ground. I never found out who they were or why they were there because at that moment, one of the policemen called to me to "Move along there."

People in the street said these Italian prisoners were being taken to prison camps.

*   *   *   *   *

Chapel End Senior School occupied the top floor of the three-storey building. Everyone was very quiet as the column of ex-third-year juniors, marched in file up the dark stone stairway, to become first-year seniors! Our little eleven-year-old hearts beat faster as we marched in file to take our places standing in the front rows of the assembled seniors. The importance and solemnity of the occasion was not lost on any of us. Our lives had changed forever.

First day after assembly was given to written tests, probably to grade us into classes. The school was divided into "A," "B," and "C" classes for each age group: A for the brightest, B the average, and C the slowest.

My new teacher was to be Miss Levene, who taught the first-year A class.

Headmaster here was Mr. Dixon, a Welshman who stood no taller than most of the boys he taught. A muscular man good at sports and gymnastics, liked, respected, and admired by every kid in the school.

"Taffy" Dixon, as he was affectionately referred to by his students, was also a Communist.

*   *   *   *   *

Aunt Lylie and my little cousin Brian came to stay with us this summer. With our dad's youngest brother, Fred, away in the army, it made sense for his wife and baby to stay with us. Lylie and our mum would be company for each other whilst they looked around for a more permanent house or flat. These two women were already good friends in spite of the difference in ages. Our mum was old enough to be her mother.

My aunt did not have a mother. She and her siblings had been brought up by their father, their mother having died young.

I liked my Aunt Lylie. She was a young woman unlike other grown-ups, because I could talk to and share secrets with her. It was as if I had a friend in the house.

*   *   *   *   *

Air raids had again become sporadic events during 1943. They were frequent enough to persuade us to sleep fully clothed, but not intense enough to make us sleep in a shelter. The Anderson shelter in our garden was now a chicken house. For that reason our mum said it was unusable, but the public shelter was only a three-minute walk (or forty-five-second run) from our front door. We never used that shelter either, but we did know old Mr. Bard, the builder, and Mr. Trotman, the retired RSM,[58] who were now wardens.

It was a particularly heavy raid one night in October. I am not sure if the noise of the guns or Mother's calling awakened me. It could have been both, added to the fact that Auntie Lylie was down from her upstairs bedroom, and little Brian was crying. They were sitting on the floor, under the old table in the front parlour. Mum shouted to me to get under the table with them, but at that moment came the whistling sound of a falling bomb.

"NO! STOP!" she corrected herself in time for an explosion so loud that everything rattled; it must have been close.

"NOW!" Mum picked up her order where she left off.

Grabbing my shoes, I made a dive for the cover of the table. My head and shoulders were well under that table

---

[58]   Regimental sergeant major.

when a second whistling bomb came down with the same nerve shattering result.

Those self-appointed experts will tell you about bombs, "If you can hear it coming, it ain't going to hit you!" I had my doubts.

"It's not getting any better," Lylie was saying. "It's not going to pass over us," she added, and she was right.

Our mum had her head under the table, and her behind with the rest of her, sticking up over the big bed! It was really a comical sight, but nobody was laughing.

"We shall have to make a run for it," our mum decided.

"George, go and stand by the front door. When I say go, run as fast as you can to the public shelter. Me and Lylie and the children will be right behind you."

I did as told and cowered beside the heavy front door.

Fear is something that cannot be described in words. Either one knows what it is, or one does not. This was the night I joined the ranks of those who knew!

"GO!" Mum screamed her order, "RUN! RUN!"

No more encouragement was needed as I opened the front door and pushed it wide open for the others to run through behind me. After opening the garden gate, I ran as fast as my legs would carry me! At my top speed, it should have taken less than one minute to reach shelter. It seemed much longer.

One side of the night sky was glowing dull red, like sunrise, and as I neared the shelter someone called out to me, "This way, son."

It was Mr. Trotman, our neighbour, the air raid warden ushering me to one of the entrances. The voices and footsteps of Mum and Aunt Lylie were not far behind me.

"It's the docks getting it tonight," Mr. Trotman said as he nodded toward the glowing red sky.

Inside the shelter existed a world silent and apart from the noisy war outside. We all stood just inside the dimly lighted cavern that was a bedroom for so many of our neighbours.

This was a surface shelter. That is, it was all above ground level and stood a bit more than fifty feet square by twelve feet high.[59] Divided into four "rooms" with four separate entrances, there were no doors, but the openings had thick double baffles, like a maze!

The whole structure, with its thick flat roof, was made of reinforced concrete and brick.

The room where we stood, about forty feet long by ten feet wide, was big enough to hold three rows of double tier wooden bunks. About three dozen people could sleep here.

Mr. Trotman beckoned to a group of women who were sitting quietly talking. Always smartly turned out, and with his silver hair brushed straight back, he looked and carried himself like the military man he was.

"Room for the Schofields in here?" he whispered.

"Yes," they all answered in lowered voices, and we were directed to four empty bunks. We had not brought our own bedding like the other shelterers, but it was nice to lay down in peace and quiet anyway. Even a cold hard wooden bed was welcome tonight.

"Has the raid moved over yet?" a woman's lowered voice was asking.

"It's going over," came a reply from somewhere.

"Towards Canning Town and the docks."

"Some other poor buggers are getting a pasting tonight."

"Yes," the chorus were nodding sadly, "some other poor buggers . . ."

As we became accustomed to the dim light, we realized most of the others here were people we at least knew by sight, who lived nearby. One of the girls was in my class at school.

Mr. Trotman never wore an ARP uniform, and I am still not sure if he was a real warden—or just took charge! It did not matter much anyway.

---

[59] Described from memory. Unable to locate original specs.

We, Schofields, became regulars at this shelter. Bunks were allotted to us, and our mum had pillows and blankets set aside for air raids.

The only thing I did not like about this shelter was the lavatories. They were smelly chemical latrines, and it was wise to use our home bathroom before leaving for the night.

Otherwise, the shelter was alright, and we soon made friends with the other regulars. It was funny to see what other people wore to sleep in. The sights included hair curlers of various designs, dressing gowns from silky satin to threadbare wooly, and slippers and bedsocks of every imaginable style and state of repair!

The few men who slept in the shelter were mostly old, and far less interesting. They seemed to favour their old suits.

Lots of the children in our neighbourhood had siren suits—a sort of all-over garment to keep out the cold during air raids. These outfits of one piece, from pixie hat to long trousers, were often home made out of an army blanket. Shirley King, from next door, had a navy blue one that her mother made for her. We, two Schofields, did not have siren suits, but wore our old clothes to sleep in the public shelter.

Mr. King had fitted their garden shelter with real mattresses, electric light, radio, heating, and a hot plate to make tea or cocoa. They ran the cable from their kitchen plugs to the Anderson at the bottom of the garden. He was good at things like that, was Mr. King.

Chapter XIX

1-2 January 1944	RAF continues raids on Berlin in spite of heavy losses.
2 January	New Guinea town of Saidor on Bismarck Sea is captured by U.S. forces. Retreating Japs suffer heavy casualties.
6 January	Russians cross the old frontier into Poland.
11 January	Count Galeazzo Ciano, former Italian foreign minister and Mussolini's son-in-law, executed for treason on the Duce's orders.
15 January	Siege of Leningrad broken by Russians.
17 January	Operation Panther, the attack on Cassino, opens with advances by French and British troops.
20 January	FDR is inaugurated U.S. president for fourth term.
20-21 January	Heavy raid on Berlin as RAF drop 2,500 tons of bombs. Thirty-five of 759 bombers are shot down; 172 aircrew are killed.
22 January	British, ANZAC, and U.S. troops land near Anzio . . . almost unopposed.
26 January	Force of U.S. light bombers destroy Jap air bases at Rabaul.
27 January	Russians clear Moscow Leningrad rail line.
27 January	Off Anzio, destroyer HMS Spartan is sunk.
Night 27 January	RAF makes heavy raid on Berlin
1 February	U.S. forces make landings in Marshall Islands. Japs suffer heavy losses.

1 February 1944	Russians cross River Luga into Estonia.
15 February	Allied warplanes and artillery destroy the medieval monastery at Monte Cassino.
15 February	Heavy RAF raid on Berlin.
16 February	Operation Hailstorm. In the Caroline Islands. U.S. warplanes destroy forty-plus Jap ships and two hundred and sixty-five planes for the loss of twenty-five U.S. planes.
16 February	Operation Catchpole. In the Marshall Islands. U.S. Marines make spectacular advances.
18 February	Admiral Canaris, head of German counterintelligence, is dismissed by Hitler.
18 February	Twenty RAF bombers hit Gestapo HQ at Amiens to breach prison wall and allow prisoner escape.
19 February	Gen. Nikolai Vatutin, hero of Battle of Kursk, is killed by Ukrainian nationalists. His traveling companion, Nikita Khruschev, is unhurt.
Night 19 February	Eight-hundred-plus RAF bombers hit Leipzig.
Day 20 February	USAAF flying forts hit Leipzig. Heavy loss of planes in both of these raids.
20 February	Norwegian saboteurs destroy ferry boat carrying heavy water for possible German atomic research.
20 February	Operation Argument opens seven day and night raids by USAAF/RAF on strategic targets in Germany.

Chapter XIX Make Do and Mend *January-February 1944*

The stone spiral staircases doubled as air raid shelters in our school. Chapel End was built a bit like a Norman fort—square with four towers. In this case, the towers housed heavy stone steps. The stairwell windows that once let in light had been replaced by heavy brick and concrete shields.

Illumination came from fixed, protected electric bulbs that were always switched "on."

At the sound of the air raid siren, we all ran from classrooms to stairwells where lessons continued. Well, we did not actually run, but marched very quickly, because teachers insisted on a good orderly retreat to the shelters. There had been no daylight raids for some time, so a run for cover was rare, and we all thought the worst of the daytime war was over for us.

We were sadly mistaken. The worst was yet to come.

My new teacher, Miss Levene, called me George. Boys were usually addressed by surname, but with two (unrelated) Schofields in the class, she distinguished us by saying Denis or George.

I liked Miss Levene. She was a cheerful young lady of dark complexion and jet black hair. Her speciality, she told us, was English, but she seemed able to teach any subject. Any subject but New Testament, that is. When it came to scripture studies, she confined herself to the old books of the Bible. Another teacher taught the rest.

Miss Levene was helpful, too. She would walk between the rows of desks and peer over shoulders to see how we were getting on with our maths problems. At my desk, she stopped to look more closely at my book.

"Move over," she ordered and sat beside me.

"Now, George," she went on in her best reassuring voice.

"You *can* do this . . . ," she said of the mathematical equations I was staring at with a blank expression.

With time, and Miss Levene's help, I did.

This new teacher also explained that the essay submitted by me on that first day of tests had been my admission ticket to this class. With her help, I was going to do well in mathematics too.

*   *   *   *   *

Aunt Lylie found a flat in Clapton; that's the other side of Walthamstow Marshes. We all went with her to see and admire the apartment on the top floor of a fairly new block of flats. She was weighing up the advantages and problems of taking the place.

"It's further into London and more likely to be bombed. But I suppose that's why it's available, 'cause houses and flats are like gold dust now!"

She decided to take it, and we all thought that was a good idea.

"We'll come to see you," I told her.

We did go there often. Even after she got to know the neighbours, we still regularly visited with each other.

*   *   *   *   *

Wadham Hall Sunday School was an important part of my "social life." with its regular calendar of events, like the Sunday school and once-a-week-evening handicrafts. We had a once-a-year outing to Epping Forest, where we would take tea at the tea shop by the Forest Hotel and play cricket and rounders on the green. We did have a lot of fun.

Did I mention the annual prize-giving day? The prize was always a book, and always on a religious subject, or a story with a religious theme. Originally awarded to those pupils with a hundred percent attendance record, there had been problems in the past with children's claims to prizes they thought they deserved and did not get. The Snoad brothers had been among those who stormed out in protest! The administration solved the problem by giving every child a prize.

This Sunday school also subscribed to "My Own Bible" scheme from children. The idea being that every pupil should have his or her own Bible. To this end, Bibles were sold to us at sixpence per copy, which was well below real value of course.

Our mum would not give me, or my sister, the six-penny purchase price. She made us save up our own money!

We still have our Bibles.

I enjoyed Sunday afternoon Bible study and was now in the top class, led by Mr. Squirrel. My sister was in a girl's class led by his sister, Miss Squirrel.

The whole chapel was in the charge of the superintendent, Mr. Cook, a big man with dark hair brushed straight back. On Sundays, he always wore a dark suit, and with his heavy rimmed spectacles, he could have been taken for an accountant or a banker. In fact, during the rest of the week, Mr. Cook was a London Transport bus driver. We, children, would wave whenever we saw him in his cab, and he would always smile and return the salute.

My sister's teacher, young Miss Squirrel, worked in a florists shop during the week. When not teaching in Sunday school, or working with flowers, Miss Squirrel served tea and refreshments to rescue workers. It was not clear to me if she worked for an organization like the WVS,[60] or Salvation Army, or just off her own bat. It did not much matter who sponsored her, for it was said that when a bomb fell, and wardens dug for survivors, there she was serving hot drinks from a mobile canteen.

My class teacher at Wadham Hall, Mr. Squirrel, was a wheelchair-bound young gentleman. He always arrived early on Sunday afternoons, giving the other teachers a chance to get him seated before the "kids rushed in." Presumably, he left late for the same reason. So that the teachers could get him comfortably seated in his wheelchair for his sister to see him home again. When Miss Squirrel was not teaching at Sunday school, or working with flowers, or serving tea to rescue workers, she became wheelchair pusher and general helper to her brother. He was a very thin man and sat, sort of half bent over, in his chair, his head always tilted to one side.

---

[60] Women's Voluntary Service.

I never thought to ask the name of his particular disability, because in his company one could quickly forget that he was an invalid. His speech was clear and his wit sharp. Always ready to laugh at the comical side of things, Mr. Squirrel, ever cheerful, would always greet you with a smile. He did not need to preach; his own sunny disposition was evidence enough of his faith.

*   *   *   *   *

As the weather cooled so chicken's egg production fell to nil. As winter arrived, Mum tried to persuade me to get rid of the chickens. "It is unkind to keep them in that ice-cold shelter," she said. "Mr. Capes will take them off your hands and he will be able to look after them properly."

I was offended at the suggestion that I was not caring for them properly, but eventually agreed to let them go to Mr. Capes. The whole business had not been a financial success, but this way I would end up with some cash.

*   *   *   *   *

Our mum got a new job, in a rubber factory not far from home, but it did not last many weeks.

"It's the hot ovens," she said. "The money is good but working in all that heat is making me ill!"

It did not take long for her to find a better situation with dryers, cleaners, and gentlemen's tailor shop near Liverpool Street, in the city. The business was run by old Mr. Supran, and his son Hertzl, and although they were styled "tailors," I do not think they made many new suits. The real activity was turning old suits inside out!

It worked like this—when a customer brought in his suit to be turned, the shop would cut the stitches to the silk lining and take it out. Same with any alpaca stiffening and cotton padding—buttons removed, and buttonholes' stitches cut open with a sharp razorblade. All the seams on the jacket, waistcoat, and trousers were slit, and the suit reduced to lots of small pieces. After brushing, sewing all the parts back together, and dry-cleaning—*voilà!*—a new suit. Well not quite, because the top pocket would be on the wrong side, and the jacket, and waistcoat and fly, buttoned right over left! Never mind, this was a time when a new suit could take all of one's clothing coupons for a year, and be poor quality at that.

Our mum sat there in the shop beside another woman, busily ripping suits. I think Mother liked the job and got along well with the other people. The journey to and fro was easy, fog permitting, because the trolley bus went from the top of our road to the shop door. There was almost no walking, and that was important when she brought work home. That is why I had to meet her at the bus stop every evening and help carry the bags of work to our house.

"Piece work," that is what it's called when you're paid by the piece and that is what Mum got when she brought work home. A half crown[61] for every suit "ripped up." Mum taught us the job, and we were soon fairly proficient workers, especially my sister.

Mother paid us for the shopwork we did. Clearing out the ashes, lighting the coal fire, and preparing the supper table every evening were not counted as wage-earning activities.

*   *   *   *   *

Now that we used the downstairs front parlour for sleeping, my old room upstairs was made the official toy room. Toys could be left lying around there, but not in any other part of the house. Mum emptied it of everything but the linoleum and two desks. The blue desk was mine, and

---

[61]   Half crown = £0.125.

the pink one was my sister's. They had been made for us by Mr. King, the carpenter who lived next door.

Mother gave us one other piece of furniture, the old wind-up gramophone, with some steel needles and a few records that had escaped Dad's conjuring tricks. These records included some Sophie Tuckers, a Sam Browne and Elsie Carlisle, and a set of "Old Time Music Hall" recordings that had once belonged to our Granny. We, children, played those records over and over, until we knew all the words by heart.

Film star, Greer Garson, sent me her autographed picture. Well, hers was one of the stars to whom I had written. It arrived in the post, after its month's-long journey from Hollywood, in one of those printed envelopes the studios used to send out by the thousands. At the time, I did not know about that, and believed Greer Garson herself put the photograph in that envelope and posted it to me! The picture was given pride of place on the toy room's little mantelpiece. With George Formby, she flanked my prized possession: the shrapnel collection.

My sister's pink desk always looked clear, clean, and usually adorned with some wild flowers (our mum called them "piddle the beds") stuck in a water-filled jam jar. I knew better than that. In films at the picture house, all the "big pots" had their desks covered with papers, so I did the same. Pieces of paper, documents and plans just strewn about, gave me a sense of importance!

Also in films, important men had libraries in their houses, so I decided to have one in mine. Of course, there were only four or five books in my collection (two of them prizes from Sunday school), but it was a start. Not having a bookcase was a problem resolved by standing the books on the lino floor and propping them between the wall, and a clean house brick that I had found somewhere.

I was by now an active member of the children's lending library, which operated out of the old Marsh Street school building in High Street. On my book-changing days, I could be found browsing around the nonfiction and science shelves.

One particular volume that influenced me was a "how to" book entitled *The Young Chemist*. It explained that anyone could make a chemical laboratory at home using homemade apparatus and easily obtainable chemicals. I renewed this book as often as I dared, and made copious notes before returning it.

My homemade laboratory was based in the toy room of course, and much to Mother's disgust. She did not like chemicals or chemistry at all. I, on the other hand, was developing a passion for the subject. A passion that would soon be reinforced with my introduction to the Frankenstein films. A passion probably sown a year or two earlier with Spencer Tracy as Dr. Jekyll and Mr. Hyde. Such was the excitement produced by the picture, I decided it should be made into a book! And I was just the fellow to write it! The project did not get very far. I had yet to be introduced to Robert Louis Stevenson. Later still came the books of H. G. Wells: *The Food of the Gods* and *The Invisible Man*. All works to fire the young imagination.

*   *   *   *   *

Chemicals were not the only things our mum feared. She was afraid of and hated mice. One night when we got home after a picture show, Mother, for some reason, put her head around the dining room door and switched on the lights. The blackout blinds had already been drawn, and a little mouse ran down the window curtain. Mum screamed, threw her handbag at the intruder, and ran upstairs.

"GEORGIE!" she yelled. "SEE TO IT!"

I entered the room in time to see the mouse scurrying across the floor, to hide under the radiogram. A big mistake— there was no way out from that!

Carefully tilting the piece of furniture, I caught sight of the little grey fellow vainly trying to hide in a corner. I caught hold of him by the tail and held him up for a closer look. He was very small even for a mouse, and his eyes seemed too big for his tiny head. This must have been a baby. I stared at him, and he stared back at me. Then, taking the little fellow out to the back garden, I put him gently on to the grass and he ran away.

Mother must have heard the kitchen door shut as I came back into the house.

"Is it dead?" she called down the stairs.

"Yes," I answered.

CHAPTER XX

5 March 1944	*First units of three Chindit brigades (eight thousand British and Ghurka) land by glider behind Jap lines in Burma.*
6 March	*Railway yards near Paris is heavily bombed by RAF.*
8 March	*Jap forces fail in fierce counterattacks against U.S. forces in Solomon Islands.*
18 March	*The Hungarian regent, Admiral Horthy, is forced to accept Hitler's demand that German troops occupy Hungary.*
19 March	*Wehrmacht enters Hungary.*
24 March	*Of eight hundred RAF bombers raiding Berlin, seventy-two are lost.*
24 March	*Major General Wingate dies when his plane crashes in Burma.*
25 March	*On Russian front, Field Marshall von Manstein is sacked by Hitler.*
29 March	*Of eight hundred RAF bombers raiding Nuremberg, ninety-five are lost.*
30 March	*Japanese army infiltrate across Indian border from Burma. Lay three-month siege on Imphal.*
Spring 1944	*Colossus, world's first electronic computer, is operational at Bletchley Park, British code breaking HQ.*

Chapter XX Digging for Victory *March-April 1944*

> *He was one of the best detectives Scotland Yard ever*
> *had. He found out what SPAM was made of!*
> —Comedian Tommy Trinder on stage

"Dig for Victory," the government popularized slogan to encourage home food production, seemed to be working, and the slogan seemed to be everywhere. Everyone was taking it seriously. Tomatoes ripening inside front room windows were a common sight when walking along any street. Some families had allotments,[62] most grew, or attempted, to grow vegetables in their gardens. I came into the third category.

A long time ago, our dad gave me exclusive use of a small strip of land beside the concrete back garden patio. It was about ten feet long by one foot deep, next to a fast-growing and rapidly encroaching mint bed. That was, he told me, my garden to grow whatever I liked, so with penny packets of seeds from Woolworth's, this became my entry into the food-producing business.

The seeds of radish, lettuce, turnip, and carrot were neatly buried in small plots, and the sites marked by the seed packets stuck on to little sticks. Every day, with the aid of a small hand trowel, I would gingerly lift the soil above the seeds to see how they were growing. This first attempt at horticulture was not a success.

Later efforts did produce some small radishes, which I ate, and some tiny lettuce leaves, which the slugs ate. The carrots were too thin to eat, but the green leaves made a pretty display, and some found their way to the jam jar on my sister's desk.

---

[62] Any waste or unused land was taken over by the local authorities, divided into small plots, and rented out to those who wanted to "Dig for Victory."

*   *   *   *   *

I am not sure how it started—the argument with my classmate Andrews, that is. Maybe the two of us tried to get through the same door at the same time.

"'Ere, who you pushing?"

"Who you shoving?"

"Want to make something out of it?"

"Yeah."

"Yeah."

The outcome of this exchange of words was an appointment to exchange blows. Playground, at break time.

Now although we were the same age, Andrews stood a good head taller than me and was a few pounds heavier. He was captain of the class football team and had a good reputation in the fisticuffs department. Later that morning, he sent a message to me, through his best friend, saying he was prepared to forget the incident. I refused.

Thinking back on this affair, I realize this was an unwinable situation for him. There was no glory in beating me, and a loss would have killed his reputation.

Word of the upcoming contest spread quickly through the boys' playground, where Robby Maitland faced me, put his hands on my shoulders, and shook me slowly three times.

"Are you mad?" he asked. "You can't fight him. He can beat Starling." Starling was the school bully, but Robby's reasoning made no difference. My mind was made up.

The rowdy mob of boys, who were spectators at these events, usually stood behind the fighter they supported. That is, the one they thought was going to win. Andrews had a good crowd of supporters around him. I turned to see who was behind me. Only Robby and a couple from his gang were at my back, and they stood well back! Ready, no doubt, to act like innocent bystanders should things turn sour.

I started the action with a lunge at Andrews. He easily deflected my left jab to the head and caught me with his own straight left to the teeth! A trickle of blood ran down my chin as I staggered back.

"Injury, injury," the self-appointed referees, always on hand at such events, were in between us dispensing justice. It was not unknown for these adjudicators to settle an argument among themselves with a punch-up. At that moment a teacher appeared. It was the duty playground teacher, Miss Cornu. (Yes, the lady from Rushden.)

There are two kinds of schoolteachers. There are those who can be easily disobeyed and manipulated, and there are professionals who cannot, and children instinctively know which are which. Miss Cornu was very professional. She put on her stern expression, waved one finger from side to side, and the boisterous, noisy crowd melted away. Her cup of tea, expertly held by the saucer with her left hand, barely rattled.

Robby's gang swelled in number and led me away to cheers. Inexplicably, a bash in the teeth had made me into a sort of instant antihero!

*   *   *   *   *

Headmaster Dixon did not always conduct morning assembly himself. Sometimes he would stand aside to let another teacher conduct the proceedings, which never strayed from the same format. Morning hymn, the Lord's Prayer, and the day's notices—and in that order. At Chapel End Senior School, we did have hymn books—sort of. The words were typed and duplicated on blank sheets by the office Gestetner, and stapled together between thicker covers. A great number of the tunes were old Welsh hymns (just the tunes, not the words). There was no escaping headmaster's origins! Most of us preferred it when Mr. Dixon himself officiated. He was usually a fun-loving sort of man who would say things to make us laugh. I say usually because there were times when the headmaster could be very serious.

Even at my age of eleven, I understood that time did not mean the same to children as to grown-ups. This was clear to me when the headmaster solemnly read the latest addition of names to those old boys who had been killed in the war. To us children, they were just names. To Mr. Dixon and the other permanent masters, they must have been faces and memories. The day, five or so years before when those boys left school, would have seemed like yesterday to teachers.

* * * * *

Our dad was posted to another army unit at Fulford Barracks, York. He liked it better there, being a bit closer to home, and we spent a holiday in York, staying at the home of a local family Dad had made friends with.

The Hudsons had a girl and a boy, a year or so younger than me and my sister, and we quickly became friends with them, and with their friends.

We saw the Minster and walked along the Roman wall, and visited the county fair. I even spent a day fishing on the Ouse with Mr. Hudson and his son. It was a happy time.

One day we, children, were walking to a nearby park. The party was made up of us two Schofields, the Hudson children, and two other little Yorkshire boys. We saw a tramp walking in the opposite direction on the other side of the road. The younger of the two little brothers, who was about six years of age, ran to hide beside me.

"It's a tramp, it's a tramp," he was whimpering.

"A tramp can't hurt you," I tried to reassure him. "Besides, he's way over the other side of the road," but the little lad would not be placated as he told his story. How he, with his mother and brother, had returned to their house one day to find everything broken. "Windows, tables and chairs and everything," he went on. A tramp had smashed their home!

His older brother joined in the telling of the event and assured me it was all true. A tramp had broken all their things!

It took a little while for me to figure it out. Their house had suffered bomb damage in an air raid. In an effort to stop the boys being frightened, their mother invented the story about a tramp being responsible.

A silly idea, I thought. She might just as well have told them the truth; then they could fear air raids instead of tramps. They did know about the war and were fond of telling me that their daddy was a soldier in the Eighth Army.

*   *   *   *   *

We did not go to the club very often without Dad. Sometimes we would go, and Mum sat with the other women. I suppose she felt more comfortable with the clubwomen, since in there, everybody knew everybody else. It was always the same people. The women gossiped about the usual things—women's illnesses, the rations, what they had seen at the pictures, and each other.

I said that it was always the same women at the club and that was more or less true, but there were exceptions. On one occasion, our mum got into conversation with a strange woman, who turned out to be very strange indeed! The newcomer was a scruffy, thin, poor-looking woman. Mum told me about her later when we arrived home. How, when our mum, just to make conversation, had said something like "Let's hope the war will soon be over," the woman replied that she did "not" want the war to be over yet. Her husband, she said, was making good money on war work. He had never had a good steady job before, and she did not want it to end!

That woman, and her husband, did visit the club again once or twice. The regular clubwomen gave her the cold shoulder. I expect she is still wondering why!

More than a few servicemen came into the club at different times, mostly relatives of regular customers. The men in the bar always wanted to question them about the progress of the war. RAF men topped the popularity list. Unlike soldiers or sailors, flyers went into action from home bases nearby.

One young aircrew member from Bomber Command had just returned from attacking Dusseldorf. He was very popular.

"Next time you're there, drop one for me," the clubwomen implored.

Men's bar talk was of the war, and the appointment of one Brigadier Eisenhower to lead the landings in French Morocco.

"Who is he then? What's his form?" someone asked.

"None," came the answer from somewhere.

"He's a desk officer. Never seen action."

"Then how'd he get all them medals on his chest? What did he do to get 'em, eh?"

"Maybe he cut his self shaving," came the answer.

We never stayed late at the club, because Mum did not like the walk home in the blackout. Our route home after dark was always by way of the main road where other people were likely to be walking. For the last few very dark yards, we broke into a trot. Mother walked with one hand holding my sister, and the other clutching an electric torch, as I ran ahead with the front door key.

*   *   *   *   *

Mrs. King next door was "doing her bit" for the war effort by taking a lodger. Her young gentleman boarder, Mr. Jarvis, was a clergyman at St. John's Church.

CHAPTER XXI

3 April 1944	*British naval planes attack and damage battleship* Tirpitz *as it undergoes repairs in Norwegian fjord.*
4-20 April	*On a hill near Indian village of Kohima, fifty miles from the Burmese border, a garrison of less than a thousand men (British, Ghurka, Indian) besieged by Japanese Thirty-first Division. Supplied only by airdrops until relieved by units of British Second Division.*
7 April	*Operation Spring. In Alpine foothills of SE France, a concerted effort to wipe out the French resistance, by several thousand Germans plus one regiment of Russian Cossack volunteers.*
8 April	*Russians advance toward Sevastopol, Crimea.*
10 April	*USAAF bomb shore defences in Normandy.*
11 April	*Six RAF light bombers destroy Gestapo HQ building in The Hague.*
16 April	*Russian forces recapture Yalta.*
21 April	*In RAF bombing raid on railway yards near Paris, over six hundred French civilians are killed.*
22 April	*Operation Persecution opens as ninety thousand Americans land on north shores of New Guinea.*
24 April	*In USAAF daylight raid on railway*

	yards at Rouen, four-hundred-plus civilians die when bombs mistakenly hit town centre.
About 26 April 1944	*In German-occupied Crete, British Special Service Forces capture the C in C Gen. Heinrich Kreipe. He is taken to London for interrogation.*
28 April	*In night exercises off Devonshire coast, U.S. landing craft by mischance clash with German MTBs. Over six hundred U.S. soldiers drown. Some bodies are washed ashore. A massive effort to maintain secrecy (for D day) results in massive rumours spreading SW England of new German secret weapon.*
1 May	*Intelligence reports show Luftwaffe had lost nearly three thousand fighter pilots killed or captured since end 1943.*
10 May	*Russians announce capture of Sevastopol.*
11 May	*General Alexander opens the latest assault to capture the ruins of Monte Cassino and "destroy the enemy south of Rome."*
12 May	*Heavy daylight raids over Germany by USAAF cost forty-six flying forts out of nearly eight hundred.*
18 May	*Polish troops raise their flag over what's left of Monte Cassino ending the six months' battle. The final week of bitter fighting cost over eight thousand Allied lives.*
18 May	*U.S. forces announce capture of Admiralty Islands. At a cost of 326 U.S. and 3,820 Jap lives. (No Japs had surrendered.)*
23-25 May	*Allied troops break out of Anzio beachhead to join columns advancing from the Monte Cassino battle.*
26 May-2 June	*Allied bombing of railways in northern France causes heavy French civilian casualties.*

June 1944	*Cruiser Bolzano is sunk in Spezia harbour by British two-man human torpedo.*
4 June	*Allied troops under General Alexander enter Rome.*
Night of 5 June	*Over one thousand RAF bombers make repeated raids on French channel targets.*
Midnight 5 June	*British troops land by glider near Caen. The invasion of western Europe has begun. By dawn on the sixth, eighteen thousand Allied parachute troops are in Normandy.*
D day 6 June	*Operation Overlord. Five army groups storm the Normandy beaches. Two American, two British, one Canadian, with smaller units from other Allied countries. Only U.S. group at OMAHA beach meet very strong resistance. Today the Allies' eleven thousand aircraft fly fourteen-thousand-plus sorties. Four thousand ships are used plus several thousand boats. By midnight 150,000 men are ashore. Allied HQ consider casualties light; today, one thousand Americans, one thousand British, three hundred fifty Canadian men die.*
6 June	*From Stalin to WSC on D day landings: "It gives joy to us all and hope of further successes. The summer offensive of the Soviet forces . . . will begin towards the middle of June."*
8 June	*British troops from GOLD beach reach U.S. troops at OMAHA.*
10 June	*Destroyer USS Nelson is torpedoed and sunk off UTAH beach.*
13 June	*First VI flying bomb lands in Bethnal Green, killing six and wounding nine.*
14 June	*USAAF Superforts, based in China, bomb Japan.*
15 June	*Operation Forager. U.S. forces advance*

	in Marianas Islands.
18 June 1944	VI flying bomb kills twenty patients and staff at a London hospital.
Sunday 18 June	VI hits Guards Chapel at London's Wellington Barracks killing 121 worshipers.
19 June	In taking Biak Island off New Guinea, five thousand defending Japs die for 524 American lives.
22 June	Russians open summer offensive towards Minsk with 1,700,000 troops, 2,700 tanks, 25,000 cannon, and 6,000 warplanes. By 1 July, 40,000 Germans are dead and 116,000 taken prisoner.
24 June	VI hits army barracks south of London. Fifty soldiers die.
28 June	Philippe Henriot, head of French Nazi police, is shot dead by French resistance fighters in Paris.
29 June	Germans surrender Cherbourg.
1 July	Estimated Allied casualties since D day at 7,700 killed.
4 July	British and Indian forces advance to River Irrawaddy in Burma.
3 July	Russian army enters Minsk.
3 July	In Chelsea, sixty-four U.S. servicemen and ten English civilians are killed by a VI flying bomb as they climb into lorries at a U.S. military depot. Volunteers on their way to rescue others at a bombsite in another part of London.
5-9 July	On island of Saipan in the Marianas, Jap C in C commits suicide along with seven thousand of his men. Among the suicides is Admiral Nagumo of Pearl Harbour fame.
About 7 July-20 July	British planes and warships bomb and shell the small town of Caen in Normandy. Many thousands of French civilians die here.
13 July 1944	In a weeklong Russian siege of the small

	town of Brody near the Ukraine/Polish border, thirty thousand German troops die.
14 July	Russians take Pinsk.
About 15 July	Four British women agents are put to death at Natzweiler camp.
15 July	WSC notes that to date 3,582 flying bombs had fallen in England and 3,582 civilians killed by them.
17 July	General Rommel badly wounded in Normandy when his car is machine gunned by RAF fighter.
20 July	A bomb planted by Count von Stauffenberg[63] and intended to kill Hitler explodes at his East Prussian HQ at Rastenburg. Hitler survives. The conspirators, including General Rommel and many hundreds of senior officers, are ordered to be killed.
21 July	U.S. forces land on Guam. In a three-week action, 18,500 Japs and 2,125 Americans die.
22 July	Russians cross River Bug. Announce formation of a Polish Committee for National Liberation (i.e., a Communist opposite of the government in exile in London).
About 24 July	Russian troops reach the Majdanek death camp near Lublin, Poland. Photos of the gas chambers and installations provide western authorities their first hard evidence of the Holocaust.
End July	A complete V2 rocket, "acquired" by Polish patriots, is flown to England by RAF plane, for examination by British engineers.
28 July	Over one hundred Londoners are killed in two flying bomb explosions in busy shopping areas.

---

[63] This officer commanded at Kasserine Pass in 1943.

Chapter XXI Here Comes the Boys Brigade, or Going to the Dogs *April-July 1944*

It was Jack Blewitt who sold me the idea of joining the Boys Brigade. He, along with Georgie Wildman, was in Mr. Squirrel's class at Sunday school. He told us about the fun they had at summer camp, and the interesting things they learned at first aid, and fire-fighting classes. One had to be twelve to join. Jack and George were already old enough, but I had to wait a few weeks. On my twelfth birthday, in 1944, I went and joined the Brigade at St. John's Church hall. The officer who signed me in said that he had been a member for over twenty years and welcomed me into the Twentieth Company of the South Essex Battalion, with a handshake, a Boys Brigade handshake, of course.

The regular company captain was away for the week, they said, but I would meet him at church next Sunday morning. The regular captain was the Reverend Jarvis, Mrs. King's gentleman boarder.

*   *   *   *   *

Our mum was, without doubt, a respectable lady. She had never smoked, hardly drank, and never went out without Dad or me. A pillar of respectability indeed, but a lady with two vices. Mother could use bad language when she thought the circumstances merited (in contrast, Dad never did). The other weakness had four legs and ran at the greyhound tracks. Our mum did enjoy a "flutter."

We got to know several of the east London dog tracks, but our attendance record was not steady. We seldom went to Walthamstow Stadium. That was too close to home, and we could have been recognized by friends. West Ham seemed to be our favourite for its clean benches and facilities, and because a lot of the regulars were women. Harringay was all right, but Clapton and Hackney Wick tended to be a bit shabby, like a lot of their patrons. Fair-weather race goers, we restricted ourselves to afternoon, daylight meets. Mum did not see the sense in catching colds, "Just to see six dogs run around a track after an electric hare!" We were bad losers too. If our mum lost badly, she would get angry and swear never to gamble again—and I do mean swear! The other side of the lucky coin showed us to be good winners. On those occasions we came out ahead, Mum would celebrate by taking us to a show, and a fish supper.

It was usually fun. Going to the races I mean, and seeing the white-coated kennel maids leading each dog around the track before a race. They used to be kennel men, but Mum reckoned the men must all be in the army now. It would be the six kennel maids who put the six dogs into six traps, as the dummy hare, driven by an electric powered motor, raced around the oval-shaped circuit. The moment the hare passed the traps, six doors flew open, and the dogs sprang out, to run after the dummy. Once the greyhounds crossed the finishing line, kennel maids threw them stuffed decoys to stop, bite, and squabble over.

The instant the race ended, three things happened. The lights on the stands went up; the crowd groaned; the loudspeakers blazed brass band music!

Our mum made friends with a few of the other women who went to the tracks, and there were sometimes other children. A superstitious lot are race-going women, who bet their bus ticket numbers, and birthdays, and never lend or borrow a pencil to mark a race card. Our mum would avoid a seat or area of the track where we had lost, and go back to spots that brought us luck!

As far as we, children, were concerned, it was good education. Our arithmetic improved as we learned to calculate "the odds" from the tote, and the bookmakers' boards. What is even more significant is that neither of us grew up to be silly gamblers.

*   *   *   *   *

There is one particular memory of a silly gambler that has stayed with me. One afternoon as we left the track after a race meeting, I noticed a woman standing by the open gate. She was young, nicely dressed, and a small child was standing clutching her coat. She stood motionless, all colour drained from her face, staring, open-mouthed with a look of either panic, terror, disbelief, or of all three. I have long wondered what her story might have been. Had she lost the rent, or the housekeeping money? Or worse, had she lost someone else's funds in a desperate attempt to recover what she could not afford to have lost in the first place?

In one way, she was successful. That girl served as a frightening example for me. I have never forgotten that face!

*   *   *   *   *

There was another visit to the club that must be noted here. It was a chilly midweek evening, and there were only a few women sitting together in the hall. Some men, including our dad who was on leave, sat playing cards at a bar table.

A young woman ran through the door straight to Mr. Clark, who was working behind the bar. Then she went and sat on a chair away from everyone, bowed her head into her hands, and started to cry.

Presently, one of the women who had been at the bar came over to speak to the rest of the ladies.

"She's his daughter," the woman explained in a hushed voice.

"They got a telegram. Their other son's been killed in action!"

"That's both their boys then," someone whispered.

All fell silent, and the dull chilly evening became even colder. Mr. Vinson came hurrying out of the bar with a glass of brandy for the girl. She sipped some, but did not really drink any. Brandy was not much help, but there was nothing that anyone could say, or do, that would help. Nothing.

Having put on his coat, Mr. Clark placed his arm around his daughter's shoulder, and they hurried out into the darkness. I did not, and had never known, the family. My sympathy was for the father. He was such a nice gentleman.

*   *   *   *   *

Our mum arrived at the bus stop one night with her usual bundles of suits, also something for tea, and a copy of the *Evening News*.[64] What surprised us was the news she had to tell.

"Everyone coming into the shop was talking about the new German pilotless planes!"

"Yes," she went on, "Aeroplanes without pilots, and they are crashing everywhere!"

We opened the newspaper, and sure enough, it was true. This must be one of Hitler's secret weapons that he had been threatening to use for so long.

We heard more, much more, from these weapons in the following days and months. The V1 (vengeance weapon) or pilotless plane was soon to be dubbed "Flying Bomb" by the government and "Buzz Bomb" or "Doodlebug" by Londoners.[65]

---

[64]   London had three evening newspapers: the *Evening News*, the *Star*, and the *Evening Standard*.

A whole new set of air raid procedures and safety rules would have to be learned. Flying Bombs, unlike conventional bombers, did not attack in groups flying together. The buzz bombs came over one at a time, at irregular intervals, and at any hour. The air raid alarm system with its sirens was not much use. There was an alarm in force, and a buzz bomb in the neighbourhood, most of the time.

The new system meant every big building, like a factory or block of flats, would have its own roof posted lookouts to warn its own occupants of impending danger. Our school had the boys, from class one, take turns to sit high on Chapel End's roof and watch for doodlebugs. Mr. Dixon and the teachers designed a system of whistle blowing to alert the whole building in case of danger. At the sound of the regular air raid siren, we all took cover in the stairwells, of course, and carried on "business as usual." Children sat on the steps, preferably with a book or something twixt bottom and stone. Those stone steps could be ice cold to the touch. Teachers sat on chairs, one on each landing, and looked up at the faces of those sitting on steps going up, and backs of heads of those facing down. Some sort of pathway had to be left free. This to allow those attending to pencil sharpening, book fetching, lavatory going, or any of the things kids find they must do when made to sit still for too long. At the sound of the alarm from our rooftop lookouts, everyone

---

65 The Flying Bomb was an "unguided" missile about twenty-five feet long by eighteen feet wingspan that was designed to fly in the direction it was pointed and crash and explode when it ran out of fuel. Gross weight at launch about 4,800 pounds including the explosive head of just under 2,000 pounds. Driven by a pulse jet engine, rear mounted above the fuselage. Max speed about 375 mph. Max range 150 miles (more if air launched). Beginning 13 June 1944, 8,000 Flying Bombs were fired; 6,725 reached SE England—of these, 3,500 destroyed by fighters, AA guns, and barrage balloons; 2,340 hit London causing 5,475 deaths and 16,000 injuries.

knew they must run for cover. Otherwise, we felt as though our days were spent sitting in the stairwell doing reading, writing, and arithmetic.

One day our school roof spotters sounded the alarm; a missile was coming this way. Within a few seconds, Mr. Dixon could be seen and heard wending his way down the steps.

"Heads down, heads down," he was saying. "It's going to pass over us!"

I put my arms over my head, which was already huddled on to my knees, and listened for the sound of the bomb's noisy engine. There was not long to wait. That doodlebug motor was so loud it could be heard even through the thick walls of our shelter. The warning was still being called down the stairs, "Heads down, heads down."

Almost at the bottom of the stairwell, and near the exit doors to the playground, sat Lenny Fogarty. He misunderstood the warning and stood up!

"All clear, all clear," he was announcing, as he started to walk to the door!

We had never seen Mr. Dixon look so angry as he ran the last few steps, grabbed Fogarty by the shoulder, and spun him around.

"A FINE ALL CLEAR, ISN'T IT?" the headmaster shouted as he pointed skyward to the source of the noise. Mr. Dixon was not a man to lose his temper, and this was a rare event.

Fogarty looked sheepish and embarrassed but unrepentant—like it wasn't his fault; how was he to know?

The rest of us thought it was a big joke and giggled. The incident relieved the stress of the situation as the buzz bomb flew on its way.

*   *   *   *   *

Only once did I actually see a V1 flying bomb, although we heard them often enough. Doodlebugs did have very noisy engines.

On this particular day, walking with my sister and mother along Mare Street Hackney, we saw one. In those days, there used to be a picture house on the corner with Well Street, across the road from where we strolled. At that moment, an alarm sounded from the direction of the cinema. I do not know if it came from lookouts atop the picture house, or Polikoff's factory behind it, and we did not stop to investigate. Mother grabbed her two children, one in each hand, and hurriedly pushed us through the door of the nearest building—the saloon bar of a public house! The place was empty except for two men, one behind and one leaning against the bar.

"What's this then?" asked the barman.

"There's one coming over," our mum explained, and the barman said no more.

A pub bar, with its glass mirrors, glass shelves stacked with glass bottles and beer mugs, is about the worst place to be in an air raid. We stayed only half a minute or so. Nothing happened so we went back out into the street again, and that is when I saw it! Flying low, directly above the cinema appeared a big black doodlebug. Maybe the deafening noise of the jet engine made the thing look bigger than it really was. There was worse: at that instant, the engine sputtered and *stopped*! I heard a scream from someone in the street. Mother reacted predictably by grabbing us kids, one in each hand, and running back into the saloon bar. The big room was empty; the two men had somehow vanished. We stood silently waiting in the deserted pub. We did not have long to wait before an ear-splitting explosion rattled everything. Glasses, bottles, shelves, chairs, tables, doors, windows, and humans shook with the blast from that missile warhead.

Again out in the main street we saw people running. From all directions people ran, not away from the point of impact, but towards it! We joined the stampede, which was moving west, down a lane beside the pub, toward the park at London Fields.

When we got within sight of the park, I saw part of a splintered concrete air raid shelter. We never knew if, or how many, casualties resulted from this attack.[66] At this moment, our mum stopped.

"What are we running for?" she asked.

There was no sensible answer, and we turned and made for home.

*   *   *   *   *

St. John's Church Walthamstow was preparing to celebrate its hundredth birthday. A display in the church hall, with all the youth groups taking part, was to be a highlight of the festivities. A buzz bomb put a stop to that.

The church hall was used as home for St. John's social events: a gymnasium and drill hall for Boys Brigade, Boys Life Brigade, Girl Guides and Brownies. Amateur plays and displays were performed here by the various church groups.

The building also served as an official "Rest Centre," meaning it was shelter for any neighbourhood people whose houses had been bombed. Camp beds and blankets were stored, and the kitchen kept ready for just such an emergency. Its use as a Rest Centre took precedence over all other activities.

It was July, and school had already broken up for the summer holiday. Our mum, my sister, and I were at home inside the house when a buzz bomb exploded with a deafening bang. Everything shook—windows, doors, dishes, and people. The centre of the explosion must have been close by.[67]

---

[66] It was years later that I learned of the destruction of St. Michael's and All Angels Church by this flying bomb. The church where I had been baptized.

Our mum grabbed my sister and me, pushed us into the cupboard under the stairs, and shut the door. We stood silent and still in the dark cupboard for a few seconds, more bewildered than alarmed. Then I opened the cupboard door with a sharp thrust of my behind, and we both stepped out into the dining room.

"It's no use taking cover *after* the explosion. The damage is already done," I told my mum.

Mother was in no mood for reasoned arguments. This was not the time for logic; this was time to panic! She pushed us back into the cupboard. We both stepped out again, by which time Mother was beginning to calm down and see reason.

I walked out of the front door to see what was going on in the street and talk with people standing outside. The sight that greeted me should not have been a shock—but it was! A thick column of dense black smoke billowed up high into the sky, from a point away behind our house. That flying bomb must have landed in Douglas Avenue.

"That's where Andrews and his friend live," was my first thought.

I reasoned that they must be dead!

*   *   *   *   *

Harlow is only fourteen miles north of Walthamstow, but that was enough to be just outside doodlebug range. Well, doodlebugs did fly to, and beyond, the village. But not often.

Harlow was the site of the Twentieth Company's summer camp. On a plot of church land, only a mile or two from the picturesque little village, we pitched our bell tents.

---

[67] The flying bomb exploded exactly three hundred yards from our back door. Destroyed some houses. One woman was killed. Forty people injured.

Our mum was glad to get me out of the way. Out of harm's way, that is. We had carefully marked my name in Indian ink, on underwear, shirts, shorts, and blanket, everything as per Boys Brigade instructions. I did not have a real kit bag but instead used Mother's laundry bag, with its "Kings Laundry" mark clearly visible. She gave me a postcard with a stamp already affixed and address printed. All I had to do, she told me, was write that I had arrived safely and post the card *immediately.*

Off to camp I marched, "kit bag" over shoulder, and wearing BB uniform with forage cap,[68] belt, and haversack. Outside St. John's Church hall along with George Wildman, Jack Bluett, and twenty or so other boys, plus a few mothers, we awaited our transport. Although Jack and George were a bit older than me, we all stood about the same height; I mean, we three were small for our age. George's mother and my mum had known each other since they were girls living in Hackney. I called his mother Aunt Dolly, and he called mine Aunt Esther. I told George about the half-written postcard my mum gave me.

"That's nothing," he said and showed me his fully addressed, stamped, and written card.

> Dear Mum,
> Arrived safely. All's well.
>
> > Love,
> > George

His mother made him write it all before he left the house! He had only to post it, and that did make us laugh.

The Snoad brothers did not go to camp. Captain Jarvis said they could not go to camp because their attendance

---

68 The normal regulation Boys Brigade cap was the pill box. Wartime shortages forced us into dark blue forage caps, with company's number (20) top and front in shiny silver.

marks did not meet the standard. The boys quit the Brigade in protest!

One member of the church congregation was in the furniture removal business and owned a big pantechnician. It was in the back of this van we made the trip to Harlow, sitting atop bags of camping gear and equipment. George's mother had given him a sandwich in a paper bag, to eat on the journey.

We passed the time on the ride by singing at the tops of our voices. We did enjoy ourselves, but I wonder what people in the street must have thought with all that noise coming from a furniture van!

A small party of older boys went on ahead to the campsite to light a fire and set up a table and forms. We arrived hungry, of course, but there was one boy who would not eat. Donald, a Chapel End boy, unlike the rest of us, did not like the food.

"What does your mother feed you on, bread and marg?" the other boys laughed and tormented him.

That night I slept well. We all did.

"These are regulation army tents," Officer Mr. Robinson told us. "They're designed to sleep twenty-eight men."

There were about twelve boys in our tent, including Jack, George, and me, and it was only just big enough. Corporal Russell was in charge, being the tent's senior NCO, and oldest boy. He was about fifteen, and trying to grow a mustache. We slept on waterproof ground sheets, and I used my "kit bag" as a pillow. I was pleased to learn that other boys' mothers also used Kings Laundry.

One boy cried most of the night. I think it was Donald. On the Sunday, forty-eight hours after arrival, his mother came and took him home. I do not think she got her money back, in spite of all her arguments with Mr. Robinson.

Mr. Jarvis organized doodlebug lookouts as soon as we arrived, but they were not needed. No bombs came this far, so the system was abandoned. Of course, there are plenty of things to get upset, or laugh about, at a Boys Brigade camp. Like the time Staff Sergeant Hunt told young Private Brown, "Take this fanny[69] of water and put it on the camp fire," and Private Brown did exactly that!

There are several problems to overcome when sleeping in a bell tent. Not least is, in the dark of night with the flap shut, the exit is not at all clear! One night a boy failed to make it to the outside latrine in time. He must have staggered around the tent pole, stepping on everybody's feet, causing a commotion in the pitch dark. The morning found Corporal Russell furious that someone had pee'd beside his ground sheet. He spent all morning angrily complaining about the "phantom piddler"! Nobody owned up to being the culprit.

I did enjoy camping and was sorry that our mum let me stay only one week. I traveled home alone by bus and train, in Boys Brigade uniform, and with a kit bag full of dirty washing.

* * * * *

Back at home, I felt very pleased with myself, and ready for anything.

Anything except the shocking news with which my mother greeted me.

"You are going to be evacuated," she said. "Next week you and Eileen are going to the country."

---

[69]   Iron cooking pot.

CHAPTER XXII

August 1944	*Heavy damage in London by flying bombs.*
August	*Rumania declares war on Germany.*
1 August	*The Warsaw Uprising.*
1 August	*Tunian Island (mass suicide).*
4 August	*Amsterdam—Frank family arrest.*
13 August	*U.S. forces reach Nantes on the River Loire.*
15 August	*Operation Anvil/Dragoon as ninety-four thousand land Bay of St. Tropez in southern France.*
17 August	*Canadians take Falaise. Americans take St. Malo.*
17 August	*German headquarters staff begin leaving Paris.*
17 August	*A small party of Russian soldiers cross the frontier near the East Prussian village of Schirisindt (Kutuzovo), and the sergeant raises the Red Flag. The Soviets are on German soil.*
17 August	*Hitler orders evacuation of southern France.*
18 August	*Canadian forces reach Mantes on the River Seine.*
19 August	*Paris uprising begins.*
21 August	*Allied foreign ministers meet at Dumbarton Oaks.*

22 August 1944	*King Michael of Rumania orders his army to cease fire.*
23 August	*Over two hundred workers die in London when their factory is hit by a flying bomb.*
24 August	*WSC and war cabinet have agreed to formation of the Jewish Brigade Group from Palestine to fight alongside the Allies.*
24 August	*A French tank column enters Paris to church bells and cheering crowds, even though sniping continues.*
25 August	*Finland sues for armistice with USSR.*
26 August	*General de Gaulle walks down the Champs Elysees to cheers—and sniper fire.*
26 August	*Units of General Alexander's Eighth Army attack but fail to break the Gothic Line near the Adriatic.*
28 August	*Allied troops enter Toulon and Marseilles.*
29 August	*RAF bombs Königsberg, East Prussia.*
30 August	*Russians take Ploesti, Rumania. Hitler's last source of oil.*
31 August	*U.S. troops cross the River Meuse.*
1 September	*RAF and Tito's partisans start coordinated attacks on German transport routes through Yugoslavia.*
2 September	*Twenty-year-old U.S. Navy pilot George Bush is shot down over the Pacific.*
2 September	*British cross Belgian frontier and enter Brussels 3 September.*
6 September	*Russian troops cross into Yugoslavia from Rumania.*
7 September	*Off the Philippines, U.S. forces torpedo and sink a Japanese transport, the Shinyo Maru, unaware it carries U.S. POWs. Six hundred Americans die.*
8 September	*First V2 rocket hits London.*
9 September	*Russians install a Communist Bulgarian government in Sofia. All members of*

	previous administration are ordered arrested.
10 September 1944	*The first American soldier crosses into Germany near Aachen.*
11 September	*Many thousands of German civilians die in firestorm after RAF bombs Darmstadt.*
11 September	*British midget submarine X24 destroys floating harbour at Bergen, Norway.*
12 September	*Besieged German garrison at Le Harve surrenders.*
14 September	*In capturing Peleliu in the Palau Island, U.S. forces suffer their heaviest casualties in a single battle with 9,175 dead. Thirteen thousand six hundred Japs die in this same eleven-day action.*
17-26 September	*Operation Market Garden. Failed British attempt to land three parachute brigades behind German lines in Holland. A Polish brigade sent to help the first landing also fails. The bridge at Arnhem is abandoned. Of ten thousand troops going in, only two thousand get back to their lines. One thousand one hundred and thirty die.*
19 September	*Wing Commander Guy Gibson, VC hero of the "Dam Busters," is killed in bombing raid over Germany.*
21 September	*U.S.-carrier-based planes attack the Philippines.*
22 September	*Canadian forces accept surrender of German garrison at Boulogne.*
22 September	*Battleship Tirpitz is badly damaged by mines attached by British midget subs in Norwegian fjord.*
23 September	*German forces "mop up" last Polish resistance fighters on Warsaw west bank. One estimate says two hundred thousand civilians die during and in reprisals after this action. About ten thousand German soldiers die.*

Chapter XXII The Third Evacuation, or Is Your Journey Really Necessary? *August-September 1944*

The little town of Hemel Hempstead was only twenty-four miles north-west of our house. On the map, that is. The journey took longer than the distance might have suggested. The number 84 London Transport double-decker red bus ran from the Crooked Billet to the city of St. Albans and took just over an hour. From there to Hemel Hempsted was a short ride on a country bus. As the travel books might have said, "The attractive little community nestled among the Chiltern Hills in Hertfordshire."

Attractive place maybe, but it was not where I wanted to be and was here only because our mum had made me!

We stood in the living room of Mr. and Mrs. Saunders, an older couple with the youngest of their grown children, a daughter, still at home. It had been arranged for me to stay with them. My sister was to lodge with the widowed daughter of the Saunderses, who lived with her own two children just a few minutes' walk away.

"Alright, then," I grudgingly agreed as the Saunderses looked on. "One week, just to see if I like it!"

Our mum promised to come back next weekend, to take me home if I did not like it. With that, I was led to my upstairs back bedroom.

As it turned out, I did get to like it and became good friends with old Mrs. Saunders. One advantage of having an old lady as a friend is getting to hear all the gossip about family and neighbours!

The bedroom I was using, she told me, was really her son's, who was away with the army in Italy.

"And what a fine young man he is," she went on, "and so good to his mother. Now Florence . . ." Florence was her youngest, the one still at home. "Such a clever girl.

She practically runs that place where she works, you know?"

I do not think the old lady was too happy about her daughter's choice in men though. Not that she saw anything wrong with Bill, Florence's intended. He was a nice-enough young man, but an American, and Mrs. Saunders did not like the idea of her baby going to live so far away.

I liked Bill; he was a tallish, thinnish top sergeant in the American army. He wore his hair cropped short, his trousers tight, and his stripes upside down. Bill was stationed near the town, and he worked on gliders. He did not fly in them, but had a lot to do with their maintenance. He did explain to me about gliders, knowing of my interest in aeroplanes.

Bill knew all about trains as well. He told me that as a child he used to live near the railway yards. They were a good-looking pair, Florence and Bill. She was a pretty young lady with long flowing black hair, and he, always smart in his uniform.

*   *   *   *   *

Mrs. Saunders would let me help in the kitchen, and she taught me her way of doing things like washing pots with very hot water and soda crystals. She was good at cooking and making pies and things. Old Mr. Saunders spent his days working in their big garden, which was all vegetables—no flowers.

One thing the old lady could never explain to me was why they all went in and out of the house by the back door! In that neighbourhood, everybody did. We walked past other people's kitchen windows to get to our back door, and other people's heads could be seen through our kitchen window bobbing towards their back doors! Why not use the front door?[70]

---

[70]   Our mum told me quietly that all country people did that.

Some days I would go to the park, but not often. It was not much fun being alone and not knowing anyone to play with. One interesting thing I noticed about the park in Hemel Hempstead: the number of big horse chestnut trees—and that would be valuable information when the conker[71] season started.

The only youngsters I knew lived at the house where my sister stayed. The daughter, Jean, was a bit younger than me, but son, Vincent, was over sixteen and already grown-up. That meant my Saturday afternoon picture show companions were always girls.

There were few other diversions. Bill would visit some weekends, but he came to see Florence, not talk aeroplanes with me. I knew that. If he stayed over on Saturday night, he would share my bedroom, but they always came in late at night and were out again on Sunday morning.

Mother visited every Sunday and came with food and things she had bought on the black market.

One good habit acquired at the Saunderses' was Children's Hour. A weekday afternoon wireless programme that I had previously believed to be strictly for little children. Having been hooked by the serial (the Borrowed Garden), I stayed to listen to the rest. "Uncle Mac" and "Aunt Elizabeth" were sort of host and hostess on children's radio, and I thought they really did appeal only to infants.

As the beginning of autumn term drew nearer, I badgered our mum to let me come home and go to school.

It was in August when she brought the news of the Hoe Street buzz bomb.

"It was midmorning," she told me. "The thing exploded right there in the main street between the Granada and the top of High Street. Killed a lot of women queuing at the fish shop, and over a hundred taken off to hospital," she said.

---

[71] Read on.

"They had to use the Granada as a makeshift mortuary!"
This was her attempt at persuading me to stay, but I still
wanted to get back to school, and Boys Brigade.

*　　*　　*　　*　　*

Our mum relented in September and brought us home
again, but it was not good-bye to Hemel Hempstead. We did
keep in touch with the Saunders family and visited each
other until well after the war.

We, children, only missed a couple of weeks at school,
and I was placed in Mr. Pierce's class. That was the top class
of the second year at Chapel End Senior School. I was pleased
to see that Andrews and his mate, both unscathed, sat in
the same class.

That first lunch time found Miss Levene as duty teacher
in the dining hall. Seeing me enter looking for a place to sit,
she greeted me like a long-lost friend.

"George," she called me and put her arm around my
shoulder. "My, how you've grown. We'll soon find a place for
you." And so she did.

*　　*　　*　　*　　*

"The Rations," that's what our mum sent me to get. "That
will be your Saturday morning job, so that I can concentrate
on ripping," she said, and that is exactly what happened.
Once a week I would take Mum's oilcloth shopping bag,[72]
our three ration books, shopping money, and a bus to High
Street market. Buying meat and groceries for the week was
not as difficult as it sounded. We were registered at one
butcher's shop and one grocer for our rations. We could
change suppliers if we wanted, but that would have entailed

---

[72] Bags and wrapping paper were no longer supplied by shops.
Customers had to bring their own.

filling out forms and re-registering somewhere else. Not that we wanted to change anyway. Old George, the butcher, and the High Street branch of the Maypole Dairy had been our butcher and grocer since well before rationing.[73] Very little decision making was required at these establishments; you took what you could get, paid your money and left!

It worked like this: meat was rationed by value—for example, one shilling and two pence worth per person per week. That means if you bought cheaper meat, you got more than if expensive cuts were taken. The amount of meat one took home, varied by the season and by what was available nationally. Our mum always told me to order "best" stewing steak. That amounted to enough for one decent dinner a week, if she made a meat pudding or a stew. Grilling or frying steaks were either unknown, or only barely remembered.

Our bacon ration came from the other side of the same butcher's shop. From the cold marble meat counter, I would walk across the sawdust-covered shop floor to the bacon table. There, a lady in a clean white coat would listen politely as I asked for "Best lean gammon rashers, please." I never got them, but always some middle cut, served from the array of sliced rashers laid out on her spotless white-cloth-covered table. Never mind, I kept trying for as long as rationing lasted.

Our weekly bacon ration was enough for one good breakfast.

Not everything in the butcher's shop was rationed. Tripe, cowheel, pigs trotters, pork belly all sold unrationed, as did poultry and rabbit. Sausages made by the butcher himself were off ration, but one had to be standing on the right spot at the right moment. All sausages came from

---

[73] The 'supermarket,' that self-service, all food prepackaged, everything under one roof, did not start to take over until the late 1940s. All retail selling was labour intensive, as shop assistants at counters attended to customers one at a time.

butcher's shops. Luckily, for us, those things in plastic packets one sees on supermarket shelves today were still away in our future.

There was no need to register with the baker, greengrocer, or fishmonger. Bread, fresh fruit, and vegetables were all unrationed and easily obtainable. Fresh fish was unrationed but usually in short supply, so if one saw a queue outside a fish shop, it would have been wise to join the line. A loaf of bread may have been readily obtainable, but all loaves were baked the same size, in the same consistency, and in the same shade of brown. White, white bread was no longer permitted. It was all government-controlled "mush."

Nationally grown fruit was plentiful when in season. Tropical fruits hardly existed. Of the younger children, at junior and infants schools, few could remember sweet oranges. None could understand the word "banana"!

Concentrated orange juice was on ration—for those under five years of age!

So many things, although unrationed, were nonetheless in short supply and hard to find. Matches, toothpaste, good razor blades (we needed them for Mum's ripping work), cleaning polishes. That is one reason Mum sent me to the market with some extra cash in my pocket.

"Use your loaf,"[74] she would say. "If you get a chance to buy anything, grab it!"

Shopping in High Street market was not as bad as it might seem. The white-coated girls at the Maypole Dairy served their customers cheerfully and politely, even though there was not much to serve. The weekly grocery rations varied a bit by the season but averaged at about two ounces' tea;[75] two ounces' butter; two ounces' margarine; two eggs; one to two ounces' cheese; twelve ounces' sugar per person. All butter, margarine, and cheese

---

[74] Cockney. Loaf of bread; head.

[75] One ounce = 28.35 grams.

were "National" brand. There were no commercial brands of anything; it was all the same, and the marg was like hard, heavy grease!

Butter, marg, and cheese never came prewrapped. They always arrived at the shop "in bulk," to be cut, divided, and weighed for each and every shopper. The Maypole girls armed with wire cheese cutting board and wooden butter paddles worked in front of each registered customer.

There was a grocer much nearer our house, but we never shopped there. Our mum did not like the man, and neither did I. He was a thin older man who always appeared to be and sounded miserable. (Our mum said he always looked constipated!) He had never heard the phrase, "The customer is always right." For him, the customer was always wrong! The simple rules of commerce sort of passed him by, and he must have seen himself as a kind of government official, there to ensure nobody got too much!

Some of the shopkeepers were also club and pub friends of our parents: Mr. and Mrs. Lyons, the High Street greengrocers, for example, where I was always recognized— and Mrs. Lyons was nice to me. One of their sons had been stationed with the army in Singapore, and they had not heard from, or of, him since the Japanese invaded. From time to time, I would hear women customers and club friends ask Mrs. Lyons, "Heard anything of your son?"

The answer was always the same, a sad nod of her head. As the months, then years, passed, the enquiries became fewer until the subject was rarely mentioned.

It was soon after the war's end when Mrs. Lyons sent me some books, saying she had heard I was interested in chemistry. Her son, she said, had been interested in the subject too, and she thought they might be useful to me. They were his chemistry textbooks.

The young man never did get home again.

*   *   *   *   *

The sports field for Chapel End seniors was a good ten or fifteen minutes' walk from the school building, and over on Walthamstow Avenue. On Friday afternoons, when it was the turn of our class, Mr. Pierce would lead the "crocodile" over to the field, there to play cricket or football, as the season demanded. Long shallow trenches with earth piled up alongside them had been dug across the land early in the war. The idea was to stop light planes landing with invasion troops. Now with the fear of German invasion gone, the same trenches served as protection from buzz bomb explosions. The older boys stood up on the earth mounds and acted as lookouts, ready to sound the alarm for the children playing games, and run for cover. In fact, only one flying bomb ever landed on these playing fields and that at an hour when no one was there.[76]

*　　*　　*　　*　　*

---

[76] Flying bombs did not make a deep crater. Unlike the earlier land mines, which were about the same size explosive head, buzz bombs exploded as they hit the ground.

CHAPTER XXIII

4 October 1944	*British paratroopers land at Patras, Greece.*
12-15 October	*U.S. warplanes make heavy raids on Formosa destroying over five hundred Jap aircraft plus forty cargo ships. Seventy-nine U.S. planes are lost.*
13 October	*German army abandon Athens as British troops enter.*
14 October	*Russian army plus Tito's partisans attack Belgrade and take the city on the nineteenth. Fifteen thousand Germans die in this battle.*
20 October	*Aachen surrenders to Americans.*
20 October	*U.S. forces start the reconquest of Leyte in the Philippines. This campaign will cost the lives of the entire garrison of Leyte, eighty thousand Japs. Three thousand five hundred Americans die on the island.*
31 October	*RAF bombers successfully hit Gestapo HQ at Aarhus, Denmark.*
1-8 November	*Operation Infatuate. British and Canadian forces land on Walcheren and open River Scheldt to sea traffic to Antwerp.*
7 November	*FDR reelected president in USA for fourth term.*
16 November	*Flying bomb launchings against*

	Antwerp continue today as ten bombs strike home killing 263 civilians.
17 November 1944	*Light carrier* Jinyo *is torpedoed and sunk by U.S. forces in Yellow Sea.*
20 November	*Hitler leaves his HQ at Rastenburg, East Prussia—for the last time.*
23 November	*Allied troops enter Strasbourg.*
25 November	*Units of U.S. Third Army enter Metz, Lorraine.*
7 December	*Destroyer USS* Ward *is hit by "kamikaze" and abandoned. This ship first saw action at Pearl Harbour 7/12/41 when it sank a Jap midget submarine.*
14 December	*Fierce storm hits U.S. fleet in South China Sea. Three destroyers are lost.*
15 December	*U.S. warplane sinks Jap transport* Oryoku Maru, *carrying 1,650 Allied POWs.*
16 December	*German forces (Field Marshal von Rundstedt) open major counteroffensive in the Ardennes.*
16 December	*Glenn Miller's plane is lost over English Channel.*
20 December	*Germans surround Bastogne trapping thousands of GIs.*
22 December	*Major General McAuliffe answers "Nuts" to German calls for his surrender at Bastogne.*
23 December	*Clouds clear over Ardennes region allowing Allies to reestablish air supremacy.*
December	*Since the liberation of Antwerp, four thousand Belgians die by V2 rockets.*
24 December	*Sixteen Luftwaffe jet bombers strike supply lines to Ardennes.*
25 December	*WSC in a trip to Athens persuades Greek Communist guerrillas to support western-backed Greek government of Archbishop Damaskinos.*
26 December	*USAAF again bomb German oil depot at Manowitz.*
26 December	*Russian forces encircle Budapest.*

| 28 December | Air launched flying bombs hit northern England. Twenty-eight civilians die at Oldham, Lancs. |

Chapter XXIII The Doodlebugs, or Let's Be Thankful for the Empire *September-December 1944*

Late September saw the opening of not only the football season but also another great sport, "conkers." In case you are wondering, let me explain. Horse chestnuts or "conkers"— those larger inedible cousins of the chestnut—found value as sporting equipment. As autumn came, and conkers fell, boys would drill holes through the middle of the nuts, to hang each one by a piece of knotted string twelve to eighteen inches long. In a contest, one boy held his conker and string at arm's length, while his opponent took a swipe at it with his own. They carried on taking turns like this until one shattered, and the surviving conker was declared the winner and a "oneser." The victor would go on competing against others increasing its value with every victory; from "oneser" to "twoser," to "threeser" . . . until the run was broken by defeat. Then the winning nut, or conqueror, could add the loser's value to its own score.

At the height of the season, our boys' playground would look like a sea of kids swiping away at conkers. The game was taken very seriously by many of its players. A boy once showed me a conker that he said was a "fiftyer." He declined my challenge to go against one of my high scorers and explained in a somber voice that he was withdrawing it from all further competition.

*　　*　　*　　*　　*

It was near time for the yearly 'bust up.' That is the annual dinner of the Twentieth Company, South Essex Battalion of the Boys Brigade. This event attended by officers and all thirty boys of the company was not as grand or as dignified as it sounded. They put up wooden trestle tables and forms in the church hall, and we gorged on 'bangers and mash.'[77] Mind you, they were really good bangers!

Company captain, Reverend Jarvis, left St. John's to continue his university studies. Mr. Robinson was our new captain, the incoming vicar was styled company chaplain, and these two gentlemen took centre place amid the other clergy at the head table. Uniformed boys of the company sat at either side of two longer tables and faced each other across an empty "no man's land." Bigger, older boys near the top table and smaller, younger ones farther down the hall. The ceremony opened with the usual hymn and prayers.

"Pass the bread," a boy called over "no boy's land" to young Private Brown. Brown obliged by throwing a piece of bread, which the boy missed with his hands, but caught in the face! He angrily returned the missile by the same means, and there followed an exchange of fire between tables.

"Boys, boys," called Captain Robinson as he tried to get between the combatants.

As I said, the bangers were very good, and a fine time was had by all.

*   *   *   *   *

It was during the blitz that a bomb hit the public house next door to the Hackney Empire. As a result, the theatre was closed for a number of weeks for inspections and repairs. That closure coincided with our stay in Rushden and was one of the few periods in my young life, when we were not more or less regular music hall goers. The other period was just after our dad joined the army, and Mother said we could not afford it.

---

[77] Sausages and mashed potatoes.

It is difficult to describe, here in the twenty-first century, how it felt to visit the "Empire" in the 1940s. Now, even the name is held in contempt by some.

Whatever anyone may tell you, whatever history books say, believe me, wartime England was a dismal, drab place. There were only a few cheerful bright spots, and the Empire was one of them. In the streets one saw few well-dressed or happy-looking people. Long hours of winter darkness added to the gloom of the blackout, but step into that theatre foyer and everything changed.

The magnificent Frank Matcham designed building opened in 1901, with seating for two thousand, retractable skylight roof, and was the first "all electric" theatre. It was even equipped with a Bio-Scope projector to show films between stage shows (or stage shows between films). As late as the 1940s, the Empire became a picture palace on Sundays.

Stepping inside was like entering another world where warm air at once hit you with a pleasant scent of perfume and tobacco smoke, and the chatter of cheerful people. Bright lights, behind cut glass wall lamps and chandeliers, illuminated the grand marble staircase.

The smart doorman would be calling out parts of the house with seating still available.

"Seats in the 'fortells,'"[78] he would shout.

At all variety theatres, it was a case of the more you paid the better the view. Front stalls and dress circle cost the most; then back stalls (the pit), and upper circle; cheapest of all was the gallery (the gods). Our family always sat front stalls and centre, at Dad's insistence.

Once with Aunt Sarah and three of our cousins we all sat in the Royal Box. It followed a win at the dog track, and our mum and auntie calculated it would be cheaper per person to take the box. That was a lot of fun, even if it was the worst

---

[78] Anglicized pronunciation of *fauteuil*; the front stalls.

view in the house. The boxes are for them as want to be seen, not them as want to see.

Entering the auditorium to take one's place in the "fortells" was another eye-boggling experience for first-time visitors. Rows of bright red plush seats faced a stage surrounded by gilded cherubs, trumpets, and masked faces. The gold relief designs continued on around the Royal Boxes and dress circle. The heavy red and gold velvetlike stage curtains were flanked by wide marble columns.

On each of these columns was fastened an oblong black box, about two feet in length, displaying a number in little red electric lights, this to advise the audience of the turn that was playing on stage. One simply referred to the printed programme to match that red number with the name of the act. Below the red number, another word could be illuminated in red letters, and it said "extra." Meaning the act on stage was not listed on the programme sheet. Well, that was true prewar, but now another word would sometimes appear. It was "alert" and meant an air raid was in progress and nervous people could leave. I never saw many patrons get up and go, but then they had paid good money to get in!

On coming into the theatre, patrons would be approached by an usherette to take their tickets, sell them a programme, and escort the customers to the right seats. After an expectant wait, members of the pit orchestra would enter and tune up their instruments. (I do not know why they bothered. Variety theatres' orchestras always sounded out of tune to me!) The conductor, last to emerge from that under-stage opening, would take his place at the podium. With house lights dim, a tap of the baton, it was overture, and curtain up.

Shows at the Empire and other variety theatres could be roughly divided into two main kinds. The older music hall style, where performers came on stage one after another, did their piece and left. The newer type of show was revue, where a company of artistes would appear together in one continuous performance. The star comedian supported by his company of singers, dancers, other comics, and, of course, a line of chorus girls. During those early years of my acquaintance with theatre, music hall style shows became fewer and revue took over as normal.

Only in retrospect did I realise my good fortune at seeing so many stars. At the time, it all seemed normal. Didn't everybody?

The likes of Charlie Chaplin and Stan Laurel[79] played at the Empire with one of the earliest revues: the Fred Karno company. W. C. Fields, Dan Leno, and Harry Lauder had also walked these boards. That, of course, was before the Great War and before my time, but I did see a few of the old "greats"—when they were old. George Robey was one of them. He was a stand-up comedian styled, "The Prime Minister of Mirth." A "stoutish" sort of figure, he wore a dark suit over a seaman's jersey and a flat black-rimmed hat, and he carried a thin cane. His "blacked on" eyebrows gave him a surprised expression. His act was a monologue of stories and comic songs, and I liked him. That man had class!

Going to the shows regularly, one saw familiar acts again and again, as they went around the circuit. Wilson, Keppel, and Betty, the "ancient Egyptian" sand dancers, who shuffled to the music of Albert Ketèlbey, were a good example. They were a nonspeaking comic team of two small thin men, and a voluptuous girl. Over the years, the men grew old, but Betty was replaced by ever younger girls. The act never changed and was always entertaining. Even today, there are club turns who have "inherited" this act.

There was once a comedian, the name I have forgotten, but the get-up and patter I remember clearly. He would march on stage dressed as a young woman hiker in shorts, boots, and backpack, with wig and large protruding bust and teeth.

---

[79] I did get to see Stan Laurel on stage. In 1946, Laurel and Hardy topped the bill at the old Coliseum Theatre (arc. Frank Matchem; now the English National Opera).

As the band played "I'm Happy When I'm Hiking," he marched along singing, until turning to face the audience and in falsetto voice would say, "Girls, hiking does wonders for the beauty. You won't believe this, but do you know only six months ago I was quite plain?"

He then nodded his head and gave a startled expression as if to say, "I'm sure you all find that hard to believe!"

His routine never varied, the jokes never changed, but the act was always funny. He never failed to make us laugh.

When Mother took us to hear Richard Tauber, I did not know who he was. There on stage stood a portly, pompous gentleman singing selections from Viennese operetta.

Austrian-born Richard Tauber escaped from Nazi Germany in 1938 to make his home in England and became a British subject in 1940. His great days had been in the 1920s and early '30s when, as the toast of Berlin and Vienna, composer Franz Lehár had written music especially for his voice.

Singer Adelaide Hall was a black American. A number of artists, musicians, and intellectuals of African descent fled the United States during the interwar years, and many settled in France and England.

This was another case of my not knowing who she was. That lady in long evening dress standing beside the open grand piano up on stage was a regular at the Empire. We had seen her several times before and heard ballads and love songs from her repertoire. She was always popular, especially with the younger girls in the back stalls.

It was years later I learned about the Adelaide Hall who, before the war, recorded and sang with the Duke Ellington Band in New York. The star had been a contemporary of such greats as Josephine Baker and Billie Holliday.

* * * * *

After all the turns—the jugglers, magicians, juvenile troupes, singers, clowns, and trick cyclists—one show is remembered above all others. Old Mother Riley and Kitty, on stage, were mother and daughter; in private life, Arthur Lucan and Kitty McShane[80] were husband and wife.

When the "Irish Washerwoman's" company was at the Empire, it was wise to get tickets early. The show was bound to be a sellout, and the "House Full" board on display.

Some people said that Arthur Lucan was the greatest dame comedian ever to "walk the boards," and I would not argue with that. His shows were always a nonstop entertainment of Irish-style singers and dancers interspersed with comic sketches. Mother Riley was not only a sketch performer but one who could stand alone out on the stage apron and keep the audience laughing.

Unlike other "dames" who removed their wigs at the end of the act, this comedian was never seen out of costume. The last time we saw one of his shows at the Empire, Mum, my sister, and I were with Aunt Sarah and our cousins. We all sat in a line, in the best stalls of course. Arthur Lucan must have been a witty man, because he could engage in repartee with the audience. Anyone returning late from the bar after the interval, or going to the "gents" while Riley was onstage, would typically be fair game. On this occasion I was sitting in my seat eating something when Mother Riley pointed at me and shouted something like, "That's right, son, don't let your daddy get any!"

I felt every eye in the house looking at me, and everyone was laughing. I sank into my seat and tried to be invisible, as I felt intense embarrassment. At that moment, I hated Mother Riley for the discomfort he had caused me.

Of course, I could have been mistaken. Maybe he was not talking to me at all. Maybe the people were laughing at something else. Anyway, I thought they were all looking at me! That was bad enough, and it quite spoiled my evening.

---

[80]   He was English, she Irish.

Chapter XXIV

1 January 1945

Nearly one thousand Luftwaffe warplanes attack airfields in Holland, Belgium, and northern France. Over 150 Allied planes are destroyed for 277 German machines lost. This action had been planned as, but was too late for, the Ardennes offensive.

3 January

Off Philippines, the escort carrier USS Ommaney Bay sinks, and later the heavy cruiser HMAS Australia is damaged by kamikazes. Later this week, two battleships and an escort carrier (California, New Mexico, and Manila Bay) suffer damage from suicide pilots. This week, fifty-three U.S. ships have been hit by the kamikaze, killing over six hundred sailors.

5 January

USSR announces recognition of the Communist Lublin committee as the Provisional Government of Poland.

9 January

U.S. forces start landing on Luzon. Japs use "suicide boats" for the first time against U.S. ships.

18 January

After a week of street fighting, the sixty-two thousand survivors of the German army in Budapest surrender. Thirty-six thousand have been killed.

About 18 January

Prisoners from Auschwitz and other central European concentration camps

	begin a brutal forced march westward. Allied airmen report seeing many thousands of people (British and other POWs among them), on their slow "death marches."
21 January 1945	Russian army push into East Prussia as German forces abandon Tannenberg. Along with the retreating army goes the disinterred coffin of Paul von Hindenburg, hero of the Great War and second president of the Weimar Republic (1925-34).
21 January	As Russians advance (RAF aircrews report), over a million German civilians join the mass of humanity shuffling westward.
26 January	British heroine, Violette Szabo, dies by SS firing squad at Ravensbrück.
26 January	Wounded in Alsace, France, is twenty-year-old Lt. Audie Murphy. He will be awarded the Congressional Medal of Honor for his gallantry this day.
27 January	Russian troops enter Auschwitz death camp.
30 January	U.S. Army launches attack on Siegfried Line.
30 January	German ship Wilhelm Gustloff, carrying eight thousand military and civilian refugees from East Prussia, is sunk by Russian submarine in Kiel harbour. Six thousand passengers die.
30 January	Premiere of German film Kolberg. This massive, spare-no-expense, made-in-color epic tells the story of the heroic German defence of the Pomeranian city port in 1807. (Over 180,000 German soldiers were withdrawn from the front and dressed in period costume for this production. It was sent for immediate exhibition at cinemas and military posts throughout the country!)
30 January	Believing an invasion imminent, Japs on

island of Borneo kill two thousand Australian and five hundred British POWs.

30 January 1945   On Luzon, 531 U.S. POWs are rescued by American Rangers in a raid sixty-five miles inland. The 225 Jap guards are killed.

31 January   Soviet-armoured forces cross the river Oder at Kienitz.

31 January   An American soldier in France is court marshaled and executed by a U.S. firing squad, for desertion. The only GI to be so punished since the 1860s.

4 February   The Yalta conference. Stalin, WSC, and FDR, when among other agreements, are promised free elections in Poland and other east European countries. Air attacks to support Red Army. USSR to enter war against Japs two or three months after end of war in Europe. USSR to get south Sakhalin Island plus Kuarle Islands. All USSR citizens in German army to be repatriated home for punishment.

5 February   Russians cross River Oder near Breslau.

7 February   Russians cross River Oder near Fürstenberg, only sixty miles from Berlin.

10 February   Thirty thousand Germans still in Buda (west bank of Danube) surrender to Russians.

Night of 13 February   Over eight hundred RAF heavy bombers raid Dresden.

Day of 14 February   Over 450 USAAF heavy bombers raid Dresden.

15 February   USAAF bombers return to Dresden. These raids plus resulting firestorms cause uncountable deaths. Estimates range from 60,000 to 120,000. One of the many British and Americans POWs, brought in to help remove bodies from debris, was Kurt Vonnegut.

15 February 1945	*U.S.-carrier-based aircraft attack Japan.*
16 February	*U.S. airborne troops land on Corregidor.*
16 February	*Jap garrison in Manila start slaughter of Filipino civilians.*
17 February	*Rocket engineers abandon Pennemünde for Oberammergau, Bavaria.*
17-24 February	*Manila. Two thousand Jap soldiers barricade themselves inside the old walled city with five thousand Filipino hostages. When U.S. forces finally enter, they find all Japs and hostages dead.*
19 February	*First U.S. Marines land, on Iwo Jima, and raise the "Stars and Stripes" on Mount Suribachi. It took over six weeks to subdue completely the island. About twenty-two thousand Japs are killed, and one thousand captured. It cost the Americans 5,500 marines and sailors killed, and seventeen thousand wounded. The light carrier USS Bismarck Sea is sunk by kamikaze attack. With an airfield on Iwo Jima the USAAF can begin regular bombing of Japan.*
22 February	*German garrison at Poznan surrender to Soviets.*
26 February	*The last of the three thousand Japs still alive on Coregidor Island retreat to underground ammunition dump where they detonate the explosives killing themselves and fifty-two Americans. Two hundred Americans hurt. The reconquest of the Philippines cost over thirteen thousand U.S. lives and probably three hundred thousand Japanese.*
All through March	*U.S. and RAF planes make repeated heavy attacks on all transport systems serving the western front.*
Early March	*Reports reach London of Stalin's*

	complete abrogation of the Yalta agreements for free elections. Non-Communist politicians in Russian-occupied Europe are being arrested; only Russian puppet governments are installed.
2 March 1945	*USAAF return to bomb Dresden.*
3 March	*Finland declares war on Germany.*
3 March	*Units of British Fourteenth Army capture Meiktila, and Mandalay on Thirteenth putting all central Burma in Allied hands.*
5 March	*Germany starts call-up of all boys age fifteen and over.*
About 6 March	*Following killing of SS General Rauter, over 260 Dutch civilians are executed.*
7 March	*U.S. forces reach River Rhine at Remagen and find the railway bridge intact.*
7 March	*Hitler dismisses Field Marshal von Rundstedt as C in C western front.*
8 March	*V2 hits Smithfield market in London. Over one hundred die.*
9 March	*Three-hundred-plus USAAF bombers based in the Marianas Islands hit Tokyo with incendiary bombs. The resulting firestorm kills over eighty-five thousand civilians. Between now and war's end, incendiary bombing raids on Jap cities will kill over three hundred thousand people.*
12 March	*U.S. Army report claims 343,000 German POWs are taken on western front, so far.*
21 March	*British and American planes make a successful precision attack on Gestapo's Copenhagen offices, killing one hundred Nazis and destroying records.*
21 March	*Hitler dismisses General Guderian.*
22 March	*General Patton's Third Army crosses the Rhine at Oppenheim.*
23 March	*General Montgomery's Canadian/*

27 March 1945	British Second Army crosses the Rhine at Wesel and at Rees, only fifteen miles from the German industrial heartland. The Argentine declares war on Germany and Japan.
27 March	Last V2 rockets of the war are launched from Holland. One lands on Antwerp, killing thirty people. One on a block of flats in London's East End, killing 135. One in rural Kent, killing a man. He is to be the last civilian to die in Britain in a German attack in the Second World War.
28 March	Russian troops enter the town of Györ on the west side of the Danube in NW Hungary. They cross the Austrian frontier on 30 March.
During March	Rifts already in the Western/Communist alliance are not being made public. Press and public announcements by western leaders make no mention of Stalin's refusal to allow elections in east European countries his forces occupy.
Easter Sunday 1 April	U.S. forces begin the invasion of Okinawa with (at first) an unopposed landing by fifty thousand men. This action will last over eleven weeks. Of the half-million Americans involved, 12,500 die. Thirty-four U.S. ships and 763 planes are lost. Japs lose 5,900 planes (including suicide planes) and 130,000 military and 150,000 civilian lives. Seven thousand Japanese prisoners taken. All U.S. POWs are killed by their captors.
1 April	Hitler moves his HQ and staff to underground bunkers in Berlin.
2 April	Soviet troops reach Hungarian refineries, and the last German source for oil.
7 April	The world's biggest battleship, the 72,800-ton Yamato, steaming with a cruiser plus four destroyers to join the

	battle of Okinawa, and with enough fuel for only a one-way trip, is attacked by 375 U.S. planes. All the Jap ships are sunk, and 3,670 men die. Americans lose ten planes.
9 April 1945	*Offensive opens against the Gothic Line in Italy by a multinational Allied force.*
9 April	*Admiral Canaris and others are executed by Nazis for their support of the July plot against Hitler.*
11 April	*U.S. forces enter the Buchenwald death camp.*
12 April	*Death of President Roosevelt at his home in Warm Springs, Georgia.*
15 April	*First British forces enter Belsen concentration camp. In spite of Germany's collapse, the mass murder of innocent people goes on: anti-Nazis, Gypsies, Jews, and anyone deemed an "enemy of the state."*
15 April	*Canadian forces take Arnhem.*
18 April	*In secret instructions to General Montgomery, WSC urges capture of Lübeck, to forestall Russian occupation of Denmark.*
18 April	*Operation Character. British commandos attack behind Jap lines as part of the recapture of Rangoon.*
20 April	*Hitler celebrates fifty-sixth birthday with a tea party—underground.*
21 April	*French troops enter Stuttgart.*
21 April	*Russian troops capture Zossen, just twenty miles south of Berlin.*
23 April	*Hitler dismisses Goering and orders his arrest.*
25 April	*RAF attacks Hitler's mountain HQ at Berchtesgaden in Bavaria.*
25 April	*Hitler appoints General von Greim to command the almost nonexistent Luftwaffe.*
Noon 25 April	*On the west bank of the River Elbe, opposite the village of Stehla, a U.S.*

	Army lieutenant meets a Soviet soldier! The eastern and western fronts have met!
By end of April 1945	*Berlin is completely surrounded by Red Army as its defensive perimeter is broken again and again.*
28 April	*Benito Mussolini, along with his mistress Clara Petacci, and about twelve of his Fascist associates are shot by Italian partisans.*
29 April	*The bodies of Mussolini and his mistress are strung up in the centre of Milan for public display.*
29 April	*C in C German forces in Italy signs surrender.*
29 April	*Operation Manna. Three hundred RAF bombers drop tons of food to Dutch civilians trapped in German-occupied Holland.*
30 April	*U.S. forces take Munich.*
PM 30 April	*Mr. and Mrs. Hitler commit suicide, and the bodies are burned by his SS bodyguard. With dying orders, he appoints Admiral Dönitz as president, Dr. Goebbels as chancellor.*
1 May	*As British advance on Rangoon, the Japs abandon the city.*
1 May	*Australian forces land on Tarakan Island off east coast of Borneo.*
2 May	*British troops reach Lübeck.*
2 May	*Marshall Zhukov accepts surrender of Berlin.*
2 May	*President of Ireland calls at German Embassy in Dublin to offer his condolences on the death of Hitler.*
3 May	*German forces in NW Germany, Holland and Denmark surrender to General Montgomery.*
7 May	*At Reims, acting for Admiral Dönitz, General Jodl signs surrender of all German forces to take effect tomorrow.*
7 May	*Off British coast, a U-boat sinks a British*

	and a Norwegian merchantman. Ten seamen die.
2 p.m. 8 May 1945	Garrison at St. Nazaire surrenders to U.S. forces.
8 May	"VE Day" in British Empire, USA, and western Europe.
9 May	Is "Victory Day" in USSR.

Chapter XXIV Rockets Away, or Victory in Europe *December 1944-May 1945*

At break time in the school playground one day, a boy came to me with a riddle:

"Two Americans are walking down the street," he said.

"One of them is the father of the other one's son. What is their relationship?"

After careful thought, my response was clear and definite.

"That is impossible," I answered.

"No, no," he laughed, "They are husband and wife!"

I straight away set out to recover my honour by catching some other kid with the same gag.

"'Ere you," I called to a younger, smaller boy. "Want to hear a riddle? Two Americans are walking . . ." etc., etc.

The little boy thought long and hard until he answered, "That can't be . . ."[81]

A feisty Cornishman—that is how my class teacher, Mr. Pierce, could best be described.

A thin short balding man who snapped out his orders as if he did not expect any arguments. He certainly did not get any from me. His ideas on education were basic indeed.

"Brass tacks," he would emphasise the point by wagging one finger at us. "The sooner we get down to brass tacks the better. If one can read, write, and do maths, everything else

---

[81] Saying "two Americans walking," conjured a mental picture of two soldiers, i.e., two men!

will work itself out," he would say. "No need for any of these fancy time wasting subjects!"

Mr. Pierce was a man of decided political opinions, too, and took every opportunity to express them. He would lecture his class on all kinds of current affairs, as he expounded his conservative views. It was said that he and headmaster engaged in spirited arguments over politics.

I liked Mr. Pierce and fully agreed with everything he said! His assessment of Mr. Churchill's war strategies, of the Labour Party's foolish health insurance plans, and of the world's situation in general sounded very reasonable.

"You are all witnesses to history," he once told us, and he was surely right, but I liked history the way Mr. Ling told it. With knights in shining armour, not khaki battle dress. Besides, what was the value of being a witness to something if everybody you knew saw the same thing?

"Nature is kind," Mr. Pierce went on. "In a year or two, you, young people, will no longer remember what a gun or a whistling bomb sounds like."

We all shook our heads and moaned in disagreement with that statement.

It was this master who warned us about the folly of spreading idle rumours. "Rumourmongers are just doing Hitler's work for him," he said.

*   *   *   *   *

In September 1944, we had started to hear strange explosions, and they were not buzz bombs. Doodlebugs had noisy engines that could be heard coming . . . and going. News reports said these new explosions (always double bangs) were gas main problems, but nobody believed that. People said these new blasts were Hitler's latest secret weapon, and would not be persuaded otherwise. They were right, of course.

In early October, the authorities admitted the arrival of the V2.[82] The second vengeance weapon was reported in newspapers with diagrams, explanatory information, and safety advice, only there was not much safety advice to give! These new long-range rockets could hit without warning, and as with some artillery shells, you heard the sound of them coming after they had arrived!

* * * * *

Our visits to the Saunders family in Hemel Hempstead put me in good standing in the Chapel End conker business. In only two trips and four shopping bags full of horse chestnuts, I was well established selling these nuts in the school playground. The market changed with the season; early on with conkers scarce, the price was five or even three a penny. At the height of the yearly craze, ten a penny became the going rate. I got into the market at eight. At one point in the season, one of the dealers lowered his price too soon. Together with another seller, I tried to reason with the renegade as he stood with his back to the outside wall of the boys' lavatories.

"Selling too cheaply makes it bad for everyone," was our argument.

---

[82] The V2 47-foot rocket weighed 15 tons at launch inc. 1 ton warhead. Fueled by 9 tons alcohol/liquid oxygen. Range about 220 miles, max altitude 60 miles, max speed 4,000 mph. Between 8 September 1944 and 27 March 1945, about 1,300 V2 missiles fired at England, and of these, 518 hit London. A total of 2,724 people died plus over 6,500 serious injuries. In Belgium, 4,500 were killed by V2s.

There were two "bangs" heard on the ground for every V2. First the explosion on landing, and seconds later another fainter "bang." We all believed then that the second one was the sound of the warhead separating from the rocket, but it could have been the warhead breaking the sound barrier. Even today, accurate information on V2s is hard to get!

"If I sold conkers I wouldn't charge more than twelve a penny!" The voice came from Lenny Fogarty who was standing behind us nonchalantly chewing on the remains of an apple. His manner displayed a confidence that was quite beyond his knowledge of the conker trade.

"What do you mean?" I asked, "Are you selling conkers?"

Lenny put on his sheepish expression.

"No," he answered quietly. "But if I did . . ."

"Have you got any to sell?"

Lenny slowly shook his head.

We, two professional dealers, turned our backs on him and continued with the reasoned appeal to the cheapjack leaning against the wall . . .

*   *   *   *   *

The clubwomen's topic of conversation this Christmas and into the New Year had been the Betty Jones murder case. Everything else was forgotten—the war, rationing, gossip in general took a rest. They could talk of nothing but the headline case and were unanimous in their belief in her guilt and her boyfriend's innocence.[83]

We had started to make a practice of meeting our mum

---

[83] In London, October 1944, Welsh girl Jones and her American army deserter partner, Karl Hulton, went on a crime spree. It ended in the shooting death of a cab driver.

On 25 January 1945 at the Old Bailey, each one claimed they were led astray by the other. Both were found guilty of murder and sentenced to death. The eighteen-year-old girl became hysterical and had to be dragged, screaming from the courtroom.

Twenty-three-year-old Hulton was hanged at Pentonville Prison on 8 March 1945, two days after his girlfriend had been granted a reprieve.

Out in the street, crowds of women demanded that she be hanged. The story was front-page news for weeks.

from work on Friday evenings to go to the pictures. People of regular habits were our family, because it was always the same picture house and always the same café afterwards. But then the Ritz Leyton always showed Bette Davis, Joan Crawford, and Humphrey Bogart pictures—our mum's favourite stars. Film shows were as usual continuous, and by the time our mum arrived, it was always ten minutes into the big picture. We would sit in our seats until it came to the point in the picture we recognized. I made a mental resolution then that when I was a grown-up I would enter the cinema before the film started and leave at the end. No more seeing up to "where we came in"!

We were Friday night regulars at the little café that was a few minutes' walk from the picture house. It was not that the "Mustard Pot" served better food than anywhere else. I think Mother liked it because the proprietress was a woman. A lady who came from Scotland with her two daughters, and they all worked in the café. I suppose Mother felt more comfortable chatting to her.

Our mum always talked and behaved as if *I* were taking *her* out. She would say things like, "Do you remember the picture you took me to see?"

When we went to eat in a restaurant, Mother would decide where we sat and what we ate, and she paid the bill. In spite of that, I was still supposed to act like the man of the family—be last to sit, first to stand up, and the one to speak to the waitress.

I never understood the charade. Maybe it was a case of "gentleman in training," or perhaps Mum felt less alone by treating us children as adults.

The police and Military Police would, from time to time, raid busy areas like markets, cinemas, and pubs. They looked for deserters, criminals, or anyone who could not explain who they were. It happened to us in the Mustard Pot one Friday evening. Police closed the approaches to the crossroads at Hoe Street and Lea Bridge Road, sealing two pubs, three cinemas, several cafés, including the pie and eel shop, and lots of people out in the busy street. Two constables came into the café—one stood at the door, and the other went into the kitchen.

"Your identity cards please," called the man at the door, as everyone fumbled for wallets and handbags. The grey-haired old officer who came to our table was a real policeman, not a special. He wore a real helmet, and the stiff collar of his blue serge tunic reached almost to his chin. All policemen, nowadays, seem to be old!

He glanced at the three identity cards our mum handed him, saluted her, and, with a "Thank you, madam," moved on.

One girl with a group of youngsters at a nearby table was less fortunate. She did not have papers, and the officers maneuvered her to the side for further questioning. Although she was wearing makeup, she looked very young, and her expression was that of someone who wanted to be sick. She said she was sixteen, and her mother would not allow her to carry her own card in case she lost it!

"If you think you're old enough to be here, you had better start carrying your own papers," the policemen told her . . . and they let her go.

Later, outside at the bus stop, our mum assured me that "She was not sixteen!"

*   *   *   *   *

Mother's employer, old Mr. Supran, sent me a message.

"There is a job he wants you to do for him," Mum told me. "A special job."

I had spoken to our mum's boss only a few times. A stoutish old man who wore his last few strands of grey hair brushed across his bald head, in an effort to make them look more. With his wire-rimmed reading glasses perched on the end of his nose, he would sit sewing with needle and thread. He always sat in the shop window—yes, right there in the window.

"It's to get the light," he would explain.

"Daylight is best," he once said.

All I knew about him is what Mother told me. That although he lived most of his life in England, he had never taken British citizenship, and now, with wartime restrictions on everything, his life was complicated.

He had been excited when the news was full of the Russian advances around the Pripet Marshes region of White Russia. He knew that place well—it was where he grew up, he told everyone.

When Mum used the words "special job," my ears picked up. It sounded slightly black market and, therefore, well paid!

"You are to go to Petticoat Lane Sunday morning, buy a live goose at the auction, and take it to the rabbi in Brick Lane. There you get it killed, drawn, and plucked," Mum explained.

"Now can you do that?" she asked, and in my best reassuring voice, I told her, "Not to worry."

She did not look reassured.

"Ask Georgie Wildman to go with you to keep you company," she said, and that is what I did—ask George, I mean.

*   *   *   *   *

Stan Martin was not particularly musical, nor his sense of rhythm anything special, but he was tall. As the tallest boy in the company, he was the best able to wear the leopard skin and carry and play the big bass drum. Yes, the Twentieth Company now had its own marching band. Three side drums, bass drum, cymbals, and six or eight bugles. I was one of the buglers.

As Staff Sergeant Hunt marched with the colour party, bearing the Twentieth Company's fine silk colours, we must have presented a fine sight indeed.

We usually "fell in" on a side street near the church we were to attend that particular Sunday together with that particular church's Boys Brigade Company. With the captain's order, "By the left, quick march," off we would go to the five base roll of side drums, led by Corporal Russell. And marching time kept by Corporal Martin and his big bass drum. Behind the buglers (including Jackie Bluett, Georgie Wildman, and me) marched the rest of the boys in three columns.

Behind the official, uniformed boys came the unofficial following of little lads and street kids swinging their arms in an exaggerated manner. Maybe they were pretending to be soldiers as they strutted along . . . just ahead of a stray dog or two!

Inside the church, after we boys were all seated, but before the service began, our colours would be presented. Staff Sergeant Hunt and two other NCOs would march smartly up the aisle to hand our flag to the vicar to park somewhere near the altar.

At service end, the colour party collected the beautiful silk colours to march back down the aisle to the street outside. There to fall in again, and to the stirring sounds of drums and bugles, march back to where we started.

*   *   *   *   *

It was exactly a quarter of a mile from the centre of the V2 explosion at the edge of the boys' grammar school playing fields to Chapel End School.

I measured it later on the map, and we all heard the thing go off clearly enough. Most of us were in the dining hall on that midday in early February. There was no damage to our school, and since the rocket exploded on open ground, no one was killed. The blast was something else; a number of boys and nearby residents suffered injuries from flying debris.

The nearest first-aid post was right next to our playground. It was like a little hospital with lots of long spotless white rooms, beds, and things. The whole complex was buried under high mounds of earth for protection against bombs, and the outside spray painted for camouflage.

It was from my vantage point in our playground that I saw the injured walking, limping, and being carried, to get first aid. Since the V2 had landed so close to the medical centre, people had not waited for ambulances to arrive with help.

One young man was being transported by "firemen's chair." Two other young men had linked hands, and the injured one sat between them, his head wrapped in a blood-soaked cloth. In five and a half years of war, this was my first encounter with wounded people, and the sight of blood was a shock! Luckily, most wounds that day were light or superficial. Worse was to come.

Within the week, a rocket hit a public air raid shelter in Chingford Road. It was after midnight and killed everyone sleeping inside. More than a dozen people died instantly. I only heard the explosion; I did not see it, but worse was to come.

Within the week, a rocket hit a factory in Blackhorse Lane. It was midday, and there were more than two hundred casualties. This factory was near the railway station we had used on that first evacuation, five and a half years earlier.

That day in early September 1939 seemed such a long, long time ago.

*   *   *   *   *

A man stood outside the 'Victory' public house in Chingford Road. On the pavement beside him was spread a flag: the red, white, and black swastika Nazi emblem. He was charging tuppence a spit.

His clients were mostly women.

Chapter XXV

May 1945	*Carriers HMS* Formidable *and HMS* Victorious *are badly damaged by kamikazes.*
1 May	*With capture of Rangoon, British control in Burma is virtually complete.*
23 May	*WSC resigns Coalition government and straight away forms Caretaker government to oversee elections.*
17 July-2 August	*Potsdam Conference. Stalin, Truman, WSC/Clement Attlee.*
26 July	*Missing Research and Enquiry Service established by British authorities to find the more than forty thousand RAF flyers still missing after air raids over Europe.*
31 July	*Jap cruiser* Takao *is sunk by two British midget subs in Singapore harbour.*
6 August	*Atom bomb at Hiroshima.*
8 August	*USSR declares war on Japan.*
9 August	*Atom bomb at Nagasaki.*
14 August	*Japan surrenders.*
2 September	*Jap officials sign surrender aboard USS* Missouri *in Tokyo Bay.*
9 September	*Japan signs separate surrender with China in Nanking.*
12 September	*Lord Mountbatten accepts Jap surrender at Singapore.*

Chapter XXV The Goose and the Rabbi, or Welcome Home *May-August 1945*

VE Day came as no surprise to anyone. We had all been expecting a German surrender for some weeks—even months. Mother had been hoping the war would end on a weekday, because Mr. Churchill declared Victory Day a national holiday.

Everyone seemed sorry to hear of Hitler's suicide, the week before. All grown-ups sounded in agreement when, on buses and in the streets, they voiced the opinion that he had not suffered enough. Some even thought he had deserved a public execution, by torture!

"Hanging's too good for the bastard," was an oft-heard comment.

The eighth of May 1945 was a Tuesday, and that night was wild. We were all out in the streets, all noisy, all cheerful. There were bonfires and fireworks, although where the fireworks came from is another of the great mysteries of the Second World War. (They could have been army signal rockets.)

Peace parties were still to come, still away in our future. Every street and every factory were to have their own "sit down" or "knees up" affair. Many London streets were to celebrate by closing off traffic and setting up tables in the middle of the road, to entertain the children to tea and cake and goodies, and grown-ups to music and dancing.

Our road quickly set up a committee to rent a hall and arrange a sit-down, table-cloth "do" for the children. Eileen and I went. It was a good party.

"Welcome Home" signs started to appear over front doors. "Welcome Home, Tom [or Dick, or Harry]," the colourfully adorned flag bedecked banners said.

People seemed to expect everything to return to "normal" right away, but rationing, wartime restrictions, and shortages

of everything would be with us for a long time to come—
1939 never came back.

* * * * *

By the time the big Sunday morning arrived, our mum
had changed her mind.

"You don't have to take the goose to the rabbi, I'll do that,"
she said.

"You just buy the bird at auction and put it down in our
air raid shelter. I'll see to the rest."

So there we stood, George and me, all dressed and ready
to go to Petticoat Lane. Mother was explicit in her instructions
as she gave me the cash. First, three big blue one-pound
notes.

"Don't pay more than £3 for the goose. You should get
something decent for that," Mum said, and she gave me a
handful of silver.

"And that's for your bus fare, and extra in case you see
anything worth buying, and you can each get a salt beef
sandwich out of that!"

Then came the difficult part, livestock sold at these market
auctions was, by law, for breeding and stock use, and not to
be slaughtered for food right away.

"When you sign the papers at the sale, you give your
right name but Mr. Capes's address. If an inspector should
come around later, Mr. Capes will just say the thing died!"

"Are you sure you know what you're doing?" she called
to me as we boys walked away from the front door.

"Yes," I called back.

"He's such a bloody fool," I heard her muttering to herself
as she went indoors.

"Such a bloody fool."

* * * * *

'The Lane' was an exciting place to be on a Sunday morning. So many of the buildings around there had been destroyed in the bombing and the rubble carted away. This left plenty of wide open spaces for stallholders, barrow boys, and pedlars of all sorts. They advertised their wares by shouting—adding to the noise of the babbling, jostling crowd.

The food sellers gave the place an exotic mixture of smells, with the scents of pickles, salt fish, and boiling salt beef.

At the edge of the market, old women sat with big sacks selling bagels[84] at four a penny.

The Lane was indeed an exciting place to be.

*   *   *   *   *

We decided not to buy salt beef sandwiches. Like so many businessmen on expense account, we opted for the money instead.

I knew where we were heading in the market. In one of the side streets stood a row of terraced houses, or the remains of them anyway. The little houses were just shells really, since the doors and windows had gone—blown out and shoveled away. Now, one side of the street had been taken over by traders. Most of them poultry sellers, most sales by auction.

A man stood on a wooden platform outside what had been the front window of what had been a house. On a lectern-style high desk in front of him were balanced papers and things. A man inside the house handed chickens, ducks, or geese, one or two at a time, to this outside auctioneer.

George and I worked our way to the front of the little crowd of people standing and looking up at the man in charge.

We waited quietly watching the sales, as I tried to get an idea of the prices and bidders.

---

84 *Bagel* is pronounced *buy-gl*; a small heavy bread ring.

It was a long wait until I saw that big white goose. It was too heavy for the inside man to hand up to the outside one. He clambered out of the window himself and held the bird aloft for all to see.

"Who will start us off at . . ." the auctioneer paused as he scanned our faces. "Forty-five shillings?"

Someone from the little knot of men standing behind us had answered the call.

"Forty-five bob I'm bid," said the man on the dais. "Do I hear forty-seven and six?"

And so on and up it went in half crown steps until fifty-seven and six.

"Any advance on fifty-seven and six? Going once. Going twice . . ."

"Three pounds," my little voice reached up to the dealer who peered down at me to confirm the source, no doubt.

"Sold for three pounds," he said, and softly, "Go inside to pay."

Just inside the doorway, a woman sat at an upturned box that was doing service as a desk. I gave her the money, my name, and false address as per instructions. She did not ask to see my identity card. Our mum said they would not expect children to carry their own documents, and Mother was right. That, I am sure, was the reason this job was given to me.

The goose was deposited without ado into Mother's open-topped oilcloth shopping bag, and we hurried off to the bus stop. The trolley bus route ran from the end of Bishopsgate to the end of Chingford Road, a straight ride home. George and I were first on the empty bus and took the front seats inside. The goose sat in its bag at our feet. The vehicle quickly filled with people leaving the market, and many carried bags of things acquired in the Lane.

The bus moved off, and the conductress came to collect the fares.

"Two halves to the Crooked Billet, please," I said and proferred the money.

The young lady took two blanks from her handheld rack of coloured tickets and punched holes in them with her strapped-on little machine.

"What have you got in the bag, son?" she asked nodding towards the covered bird on the deck.

"A goose," I answered truthfully.

"You know you're not supposed to carry animals on a bus?"

George and I put on our surprised expressions as though we had never even suspected such a rule existed.

"Hold it tight," she added.

I was right in thinking she had a kind face. Our lady conductress moved on without taking the matter further.

Our tightly packed standing-room-only trolley bus was moving along nicely when we decided to check the cargo. George lifted the bag a few inches, as I cautiously opened it. The goose's head on top of its long neck quickly arose out of the bag to reach my face level. There we froze for a second or two, face to beak. Then it bit me hard on the lip. Taken by surprise, I lost my grip on the shopping bag, and in that instant, the goose was out of the bag and trying to fly! It is not clear who was more shocked and excited: the other passengers, or me and George, or the goose.

It seemed longer than the few seconds it actually took for pandemonium and shouting to cease, and with other people's help, for the goose to be replaced in its shopping bag.

Back at home, George and me did not mention this incident to Mother.

*   *   *   *   *

Bill and Florence came to our house to tea. They had spent most of the day together in London before meeting our mum at the tailor shop to travel home with her on the trolley bus. They sat in the front seats upstairs on the 557 electric bus, so that Bill could see something of London on the hour-long ride.

Judging by the way she always spoke, our mum did not really like Yanks. I reasoned that it was because she saw only the worst ones as she looked out of her tailor's shop window in the City.[85] Bill was the exception; she liked him. Walking to the house, Bill admired our road because of the green hedges around all the front gardens. Mum said that she thought it was not what he had expected. As I opened the front door to let them in, the voice of Damian Snoad could be heard as he ran to his front door.

"Mum, Mum," he shouted.

"Mrs. Schofield's got a real live Yank in her house!"

It was a nice visit that gave me the chance to show Bill where I lived, and Mother had bought some black-market delicacies for the tea table. In answer to a question from our mum, Bill told us his home was in Ohio. I do not think that meant much to her. She had only heard of Hollywood and Texas!

Florence told us of their plans to marry in the USA. I was not surprised. She was working on the American accent already.

*   *   *   *   *

Mother did keep her promise to let me go with her to the rabbi, but not with the goose. That badly behaved animal she took by herself, but I went along next time when she carried two chickens for her employer.

The rabbi was housed in an old building in, or near, Brick Lane. We—that is, Mum, my sister, and I—walked from Liverpool Street station carrying the birds.

A thin, black-bearded man stood at one end of a room. He was dressed completely in black from hat to boots, and a

---

[85] The shop was nearly opposite "Dirty Dick's," a tavern popular with American servicemen.

blood-and-feather-splattered long black apron covered the front of his clothes.

A woman, who looked in charge, took the chickens from our mum and handed them one at a time to the man in black. He cut each bird's throat by sticking a small knife blade under the upper beak, saying a prayer as he did so. At the side of the room and to the rabbi's right was a heavy concrete table with holes in the top. The circular holes, wide at the top, narrower at the bottom, were big enough to hold a dying chicken with its head down and tail up. There the birds stayed long enough, I suppose, to let the blood drain out of their bodies!

Customers were coming and going, and at the other end of the room women sat on chairs busily plucking and cleaning the poultry from the concrete table. Everyone seemed cheerful as they chatted and went about their duties. As we looked on, one of the women workers drew an egg from the chicken she was cleaning . . . Then another, and another. The eggs were all soft shelled and each one smaller than the one before. The excited woman called the attention of the customer whose property they were.

Outside in the street, Mum remarked on the honesty of that worker. As Mum pointed out to me, "She could have kept the eggs and said nothing!"

* * * * *

Headmaster Dixon decided that Chapel End Senior School should, as an educational exercise, have its own general election ahead of the real elections.[86] Four teachers volunteered (or were conscripted) to organise the election

---

[86] Mr. Churchill's wartime coalition government announced national elections to be held of 5 July 1945, but ballots would not be counted and winners named until 26 July. This delay to allow military personnel overseas' votes to be included at the same time.

of four candidates for the four major political parties. I was elected the Conservative Party candidate.

We scrounged literature from the real party offices, painted posters, made speeches, and organized meetings, which, in my case, were poorly attended, and even my own agent resigned. He explained to me that he only agreed to be a Conservative because nobody else in his class wanted to. Now that I was the official candidate, he was going back to being a Labour supporter.

On the morning of our elections, the whole school assembled in the hall and sat on the floor, in class lines. Headmaster led the school in a singsong as they waited impatiently for the ballots to be counted. I shall always remember the results as they went up on the board.

C. Briggs	Labour	273
B. Ayton	Liberal	36
G. Schofield	Conservative	16
J. Grey	Communist	12
Spoiled Ballots		1

West Walthamstow was indeed a solid Labour constituency. It was without doubt a "safe seat" for Clement Attlee's party.

*   *   *   *   *

I was at Boys Brigade camp in Marlow in August when news of the two atom bombs and Japan's surrender were announced. Nobody had ever heard of an atom bomb, and we did not know what it was!

The boy who was explaining it all to us said the explosive parts were no bigger than golf balls, but powerful enough to destroy a whole big city! It sounded wonderful. Just to think that the war could end so quickly, and without casualties.

Some of the older boys showed disappointment at war's swift end. They had hoped to get into the forces and the fighting before it was over.

"Not to worry," was the consoling advice going around camp, as the optimists predicted, "There's bound to be another war before long."

*   *   *   *   *

Our dad was among the first to be demobilised ("demobed"). He was still a private in the RASC. In those days, a soldier was awarded one little bright red chevron for every year of war service. These tiny upside-down stripes were worn at the bottom of the sleeve. Private Schofield had five of these, because First World War time counted.

The government decided that every serviceman should be issued with a new "civvy" suit, shirt, shoes, tie, and trilby hat. With that, and a cash grant that depended on his rank and years of service, he was ready for "civvy street."

It was not that the clothes were poor quality. It was that they were all of similar designs and patterns. Any man wearing a demob suit could be immediately picked out as wearing a demob suit.

Dad arrived home unannounced, in the very early hours of the morning. He did not have his door key and tried to awaken our mum by throwing stones at the upstairs bedroom windows. When that failed, he tried to open the downstairs windows, before knocking at the front door.

An old lady who lived on the other side of the road called the police . . .

EPILOGUE

Our dad's business did not last long after war's end. So many of his old customers had been "bombed out" or moved away. Competitors had started to move in, and he was broke within a year. He spent the last days of his working life at a local factory.

Dad and Mum lived on at the same house until they died within a few months of each other, of natural causes, and at an advanced age.

My sister moved to Sussex after her wedding. Now a widow, she is still there.

Greatuncle Alf, an air raid warden all through the bombing, was the nearest our family had to a war hero. He was still a bachelor after the war, when in his midfifties he married a widow, who died a couple of years later. When last seen, he was remarried and had a pub in Chelmsford.

The area around old Maidstone Street, Shoreditch, was never rebuilt and is today a green park and children's recreation area. The Goldsmiths Arms public house is gone, and a new building stands in its place. Remember Aunt Edie, the girl whose wedding day was spoiled by the outbreak of hostilities? Well, after the war, she and her husband became governor and missus of the "Goldsmiths," for a while. Hers was not a happy life, as she suffered ill health most of the time; grossly overweight, she was housebound, then bedridden for the last years of her life.

The Crooked Billet (and the club) was demolished to make way for road widening and a flyover.

On a visit to Walthamstow, I went to see Chapel End School only to find a deep hole in the ground. The building had fallen victim to a Department of Education reorganization plan.

With the growing popularity of television after the war, almost all of the variety theatres went out of business, as did most cinemas. The Hackney Empire became a bingo hall, then a television studio for a few years. The old building still stands, and subsidised variety shows are still performed. The Walthamstow Palace, after the war, housed a repertory theatre company, then a bingo club, then a warehouse, before being demolished to make way for shops.

The building housing the Granada is still in Hoe Street, but it looks dirty and abandoned, like the neighbourhood around it.

In 1954, Old Mother Riley (Arthur Lucan) died backstage waiting to go on at a North Country music hall (the Tivoli, Hull). He was old, alone, bankrupt, and trying to pay a heavy tax bill. A plaque marks the spot where he died. To this day, there exists an active Old Mother Riley, Arthur Lucan Appreciation Society.

Florence sailed to the USA at war's end, but did not marry Bill! In a letter to her parents, she explained that Bill had not come to meet her at the station, and back with his own family, and in civilian clothes, he was not the clean-cut handsome young soldier she had known in England. She stayed on, in another part of the country, met and married another young man.

Old Mr. and Mrs. Saunders had one last tragedy to bear when their seventeen-year-old grandson was badly hurt by a bomb. Vincent, with a group of pals, found an unexploded bomb . . . and exploded it.

* * * * *

I last heard of Miss Levene about 1963. A rabbi's daughter, she was teaching Jewish children in a poor East End neighbourhood.

*   *   *   *   *

The third of October 2000 marked the sixtieth anniversary of the first bombing of Rushden. More than a hundred people assembled at the war memorial to commemorate the event. They came from as far as Colchester, Cambridge, and London, and some were veterans of those early war days. The headmaster, with children from Alfred Street School, attended, and after a two-minute silence, flowers were laid at the memorial.[87]

---

[87] This story was related to me by Eric Fowell in private correspondence.

Estimates of the total number of people killed in the Second World War vary greatly and must be taken as very approximately between forty and sixty million.

Total Deaths* As Direct Result of War

American	360,000
Australian	30,000
British	390,000
Canadian	40,000
Chinese**	1,500,000
Czech	220,000
Dutch	250,000
French	550,000
Finn	85,000
German	4,500,000
Greek	415,000
Hungarian	485,000
Indian	36,000
Italian	400,000
Japanese	2,000,000

---

*   *Includes concentration and prison camp deaths.*
** *Not including the uncountable number of civilians.*

Jews (of all nations)	6,000,000
Polish	6,000,000
Rumanian	500,000
Soviets	20,000,000
Yugoslavs	1,500,000

Some statistics on war casualties by nation:

Poland suffered the greatest number of casualties as a percentage of total population losing 25 percent of its people.

Of Greece's 260,000 civilians to die, half were resistance fighters.

Of Americans killed in action, nearly 40 percent were aviators of some sort. Less than ten thousand were civilians.

Of Germany's three-and-a-half million military dead, 80 percent died on the Russian front.

For historical background, the following publications were among those consulted:

Burma: The Longest War 1941-45	Lewis Allen
Second World War, 6 Vol.	Winston S. Churchill
V2	Walter Dornberger
Crusade in Europe	Dwight Eisenhower
The Second World War	Martin Gilbert
Hitler's Willing Executioners	Daniel Jonah Godhagen
Hackney at War	Jennifer Golden
Churchill and Roosevelt:	
The Complete Correspondence, 2 Vol.	Ed. Warren F. Kimball
Memoirs	Bernard Montgomery
The Rising Sun in the Pacific 1931-	
April 1942 (and other works)	Samuel Eliot Morison

The Rise and Fall of the Third Reich	William L. Shirer
History of England 1914-45	AJP Taylor
The Spanish Civil War	Hugo Thomas
Russia at War 1941-45	Alexander Werth
Rhineland: The Battle to End the War	
(and other works)	Denis Whitaker
The War Over Walthamstow	Ross Wyld

Jane's Fighting Ships

The many HMSO, Ministry of
 Home Security, and Civil Defence
 Publications

The BBC Web sites

The Walthamstow Guardian

The Walthamstow Post

The Hackney Gazette

The Rushden Echo and Argus

The Risdene Echo

The Daily Express

The New York Times

The author would like to thank Norma;
and

Michael Kirkland at Hackney Archives Department;
Brian Mardall at Vestry House Museum, Walthamstow;
Eric Fowell, Roy Presland, Andrew Presland;
The Rushden and District History Society;
The helpful ladies at Cyrenius H. Booth Library, Newtown,
Connecticut;

And to all those who, over the years, were patient enough
to share their war experiences with me: British,
Commonwealth, American soldiers, sailors, airman, and
civilians. Germans, Nazi, and otherwise. Italians, Fascist, and
otherwise. French, Russian, Pole, and Japanese.
Concentration camp victims. Heroes, workers, shirkers, and
black market dealers. People who, though they may not be
named in this, or any other book, contributed to the making
of this story.

Photograph of author by Miriam Berkley.

Cover painting by Duane Gillogly.